Police in Nazi Germany

Police in Nazi Germany

PAUL GARSON

AMBERLEY

The Laughing Policemen
A group of policemen have apparently
been amused by something happening
off-camera. Two are seen wearing
sports badges and ribbon bars that
give evidence to a pre-war time frame.

First published 2019

Amberley Publishing
The Hill, Stroud
Gloucestershire, GL5 4EP

www.amberley-books.com

Copyright © Paul Garson 2019

The right of Paul Garson to be identified as the Author
of this work has been asserted in accordance with the
Copyright, Designs and Patents Act 1988.

British Library Cataloguing in Publication Data.
A catalogue record for this book is available from the British Library.

ISBN 978 1 4456 8716 2 (print)
ISBN 978 1 4456 8717 9 (ebook)

Origination by Amberley Publishing.
Printed in Great Britain.

Contents

Preface   6

Introduction to the Nazi Police State   8

Pre-Third Reich Roots – The Men in the Shako Helmets   21

Transition – Serving the Swastika   35

Family Ties – Separation of Duties   39

Police Organisations – Conscripts of the Police State   48

Aktions in the Field – Eastern Europe and Russia   84

The Beginning of the End   109

Post-Mortem – Death Cards, Justice and Retribution   121

Suggested Reading and Select Bibliography   127

About the Author   128

Preface

They originally came from Germany's big city police forces where they had previously dealt with traffic control, street crime, and the often violent street demonstrations occurring during Germany's political turmoil of the 1920s. They shared their longstanding police traditions and comradeship and held the safety and security of their homeland at heart. When orders were given, they complied.

With the rise to power of the Nazi Party and the assimilation of the German police formations under Himmler's SS and military control, many members would fight and die in combat on both the Eastern and Western Fronts, either in anti-Partisan actions or front line engagements with Allied forces. Others would guard railways, industrial installations, patrol city streets and enforce ordnances and state edicts.

Some would also take part in 'The Holocaust by Bullets,' the face-to-face murder of over 1 million men, women and children. After the war's end, many returned to their civilian police roles, concealing their complicity in the Holocaust. Very few were ever brought to justice.

The photographs seen here – most one of a kind originals and in the author's personal collection – were selected after an extended search and examination of over 500,000 images. Each was chosen for both its intrinsic photographic composition and historical context; each an instant of time recorded within the twelve-year lifespan of the Third Reich, including the six years of the Second World War as it swept through Europe in an era that shook civilization to its foundations. The photographs, resurfacing decades later, were sourced from over twenty countries, and in most part were taken by 'ordinary' soldiers wearing the uniform of Nazi Germany and often gazing through the apparently ubiquitous personal cameras they had taken to war to record their experiences. While mere small slips of paper imprinted with often faded black and white images, they carry the weight of historical documentation now helping to shed light on those darkest of times.

Disclaimer: No accusations of war crimes are attached to any of the individuals seen in this volume, except where documented as such. It should be noted that some of the first to resist the rise of National Socialism were four policemen killed during the infamous 8–9 November 1923 Munich 'Beer Hall Putsch' when Hitler led a failed Nazi attempt to overthrow the government. The officers were Fredrich Fink, Nikolaus Hollweg, Max Schobert and Rudolf Schraut. Today a plaque records their names, replacing the Nazi era memorial praising the Nazi followers who died during the event.

German Police
Transitional imagery appearing on a commercial postcard graphically illustrates the absorption of the civilian police force by Himmler's SS monolith. The traditional shako helmet gives way to the military *Stahlhelm* steel helmet. Though drawn from different generations, both policemen have been depicted with piercing blue Aryan eyes.

Before and After – Hamburg
A civilian policeman has put aside his traditional civilian police uniform for that of the German Wehrmacht and now wears the collar insignia of a NCO or sergeant.

Introduction to the Nazi Police State

The long history of the German police and constabulary has earned them the accolade as 'one of the most efficient law enforcement agencies in the history of man'. The German public in general respected and supported the police as their protectors, in part a function of the ingrained cultural affinity nearing the level of reverence afforded male authority figures. The resulting subjugation, subversion and ultimate perversion of the police authority by the Nazi Party and its leaders saw the German police tradition tarnished with a criminality far greater in scope and perfidy than any of the criminals it had previously pursued.

Nazi Germany as a police state set about reorganising its cadres of policemen, a plethora of organisations now tasked with implementing the new world order both within the borders of the Greater Reich and the conquered territories.

The civilian policemen 'assimilated' into the Third Reich's paramilitary vision of a state police force were often middle-aged, not particularly politically minded, much less fanatical National Socialists, but with the rise to dominance of the Nazi Party in January 1933 and Himmler's SS ideology of state-sponsored terror, they were 'politicised' and absorbed by the power structure, eventually turning in their distinctive shako helmets for the steel helmet and the uniform of the German military.

In 1936 the uniformed national police *Ordnungspolizei* (aka Orpo) or Order Police took form as the result of a German Interior Ministry decree under the aegis of *Reichsführer-SS* Himmler as part of his overall plan to create his vision of a utopian SS police state. It followed that in 1937 *Reichsminister* Himmler established regional representatives for all SS and police agencies. Known as the Higher SS and Police Leaders (*Höhere SS- und Polizeiführer* or HSSPF), it represented the pantheon of interests attributed to the SS and police, including police functions, settlement planning, caring for ethnic Germans and supervising the maintenance of the military wing of the SS – the Waffen-SS. By 1938 SS officers were in charge of all uniformed police forces and found that the overwhelming majority of police officers welcomed the assimilation, which itself greatly increased their policing powers as well as their personal prestige.

First formed in 1939, the *Feldgendarmerie* were charged with several tasks, including maintaining military order, traffic control and road security, hunting downed Allied airmen, arresting deserters, the collection of prisoners and anti-partisan actions, which often resulted in 'collateral' civilian deaths. They, as well as other police units, earned a special enmity from the Red Army, who placed a bounty on their heads.

Also established in July 1939, the *Geheime Feldpolizei* (GFP), or Secret Military Police, was initially charged with investigating acts of espionage and sabotage, treasonable activities, murder, black marketeering and other crimes within the military. It also worked in conjunction with other German security forces in the murder of Jews and execution of partisans, as well as the killings of hostages and other 'enemies' of Nazi Germany. Members often wore civilian clothing rather than uniforms.

The responsibility for the maintenance of order in cities and larger towns went to the *Schutzpolizei*, while the *Gendarmerie* watched over the rural areas, pursued poachers and served as Alpine homeland defence troops. The previously mentioned *Orpo* (Order Police) pursued general law enforcement, while detectives of the *Kriminalpolizei* (Kripo) pursued offenders of more serious and violent crimes. The *Sicherheitspolizei* (SiPo) was staffed by members of the *Geheime Staatspolizei* (aka Gestapo, or Secret State Police) and the *Sicherheitsdienst* (SD). In 1942, the Kripo, SD and Gestapo were all combined under the authority of the *Reichssicherheitshauptamt* (RSHA).

Even firefighters, both professional and volunteer, became *Feuerschutzpolizei* and also 'nationalised and police-centric' under the umbrella of the *Ordnungspolizei* in 1938. As Allied bombing set Germany's cities ablaze, some 2 million fought the firestorms. An adjunct of bombing defence was the Air Civil Defence Force or *Luftschutzpolizei*, who dealt with air-raid alerts, security, emergency service and the rescue of victims.

A Plethora of *Polizei*

Additional subdivisions included the *Gesundheitspolizei* (Health Police), *Gewerbepolizei* (Commercial or Trade Police) and the *Baupolizei* (Building Police). Other police entities included the *Verkehrspolizei* (Traffic Police), which also served as escorts for top-level Nazi officials when motoring about Germany. The *Wasserschutzpolizei* guarded the coasts, rivers, harbours and ports. Formed in 1937, the *Grenz-Polizei* (G-P, or Frontier Police) was charged with guarding Germany's borders, but was disbanded in 1941 as the Third Reich expanded beyond its original frontiers.

Specialists in dealing with labour protests, strike-breaking and dealing with any potential civil uprisings were the *Technische Nothilfe* (aka TeNo, or Technical Emergency Corps), counting over 100,000 members by 1943. Meanwhile, the *Funkschutz*, or Radio Guards, were assigned the security of radio stations. They also kept vigil for any illegal reception of foreign radio broadcasts – a serious crime in the Third Reich. Occasionally mistaken for SS soldiers because they donned surplus black uniform tunics, the *Werkschutzpolizei* provided factory building security as night watchmen.

Yet another organised police unit was the Forest Police, introduced in late 1939 as the paramilitary security formation the *Forstschutzkommando* (FSK), or known simply as *Forstschutz*. A volunteer formation of some 10,000 members, principally forestry officials and forest workers, its overall commander was the avid huntsman and Luftwaffe leader *Reichsmarshall* Hermann Göring. Only briefly trained, they were initially sent to Poland's forests to combat poachers, wood thieves and to supply security for lumber transport.

However, they also took part in actions following the 1941 order to make ready the famous ex-Czarist hunting preserve of the Białowieża Forest for Göring's personal hunting plans. The police units saw to the expulsion of the Polish residents, their lands and farms being destroyed in the process, as were two small Jewish communities. A year later the poorly prepared *Forstschutz* were sent to the Ukraine to meet the partisan threat, during which they incurred many losses.

Facing less danger, the *Forstschutz* also took a significant part in the hunting and killing of unarmed Jews, particularly those hiding in the forests. They also took over the execution duties of the SS and police when needed. As the Allies advanced on Nazi Germany, *Forstschutz* personnel found themselves facing more of a combat infantry role.

Colour Coded

While the photographic images invariably are in black and white, in reality the variegated list of colours employed to identify the various militarised police formations include police green for the *Schutzpolizei des Reich*, orange for the *Wasserschutzpolizei* (Water Police), crimson red (*karesinrot*) for the *Feuerschutzpolizei* (Firemen), cornflower blue for the *Polizei Medizinal Beamte* (Police Medical Department), light grey for the *Polizei Veterinar Beamte* (Veterinarian Police) and wine red for the *Schutzpolizei des Gemeinden* (Secret Field Police). White shoulder straps were worn by the Motorised Gendarmerie Emergency Units, with these officers patrolling the German autobahns. In wartime, the wine red of the Secret Field Police was supplanted with police green as the two merged into the *Schutzpolizei des Reich*. The *Schutzpolizei* (Protection Police) were charged with regular police duties in pre-Third Reich Germany before being incorporated into the SS, where they took part in anti-partisan warfare and, upon entry into Eastern Europe, the mass executions of 'racial enemies of the state'.

The War Within a War

Reichsmarshall Hermann Göring, often described as congenial and charming, in addition to being one of the closest confidants of Hitler and a pivotal founder of the Nazi state, wielded power as commander of the German Luftwaffe, President of the Reichstag and as Prime Minister

Like-Minded
Civilian Party members, Nazi officials and policemen gather at the Hermann Göring Police Regimental Centre. In the centre and staring into the camera is a member of the RLB (*Richsluftschutzbund*), the paramilitary State Air Protection Group charged as of 1933 with directing air-raid protection and civil defence programs.

of Prussia. He was also the creator of the Gestapo and Dachau, the first concentration camp, and was the individual who directed SS Security Police Reinhard Heydrich to implement the Final Solution. In describing Germany's avowed purpose for waging war, Göring stated: 'This war is not the Second World War. This is the great racial war. In the final analysis it is about whether the German and Aryan prevails here, or whether the Jew rules the world, and that is what we are fighting for out there.'

Another Nazi potentate, *Reichsführer* Heinrich Himmler, head of the SS, while giving a speech on 4 October 1943 on the occasion of a convention of SS Major Generals in Posen, praised the mass killings of Jews, calling it a 'glorious page in our history':

> I wish to speak to you here publicly, and for all to hear, about a very difficult subject. It should be discussed among our own ranks very openly, though we shall never speak about it in public. Just as little as we hesitated on June 30, 1934 to do what duty commanded, and line comrades who had transgressed up against the wall to be shot, we have never spoken about these matters. Nor will you ever speak about them. It was, thank God, a natural tactfulness deep within us which has motivated us to keep our silence on these topics in conversation, never to speak about them. Each and every one of us has shuddered at their thought, yet each of us was certain that he would do it again, if necessity so demanded and orders so required. What I am referring to is the evacuation of the Jews, the extermination of the Jewish people. This is one of those things that are so easily said. 'The Jewish people is being exterminated,' says every Party member. 'Of course, it's in our Party programme – excluding the Jews, extermination. We're taking care of it.' And then there they are, those good, upstanding 80 million Germans. And each one of them has a fine, decent Jew whom he knows well. Of course, it's obvious, the others are all pigs – but this Jew, he's OK, a great guy. All those who talk like this – none of them has looked on and watched, none has endured it. Most of you will know what it means if a hundred bodies are piled high, five hundred or a thousand. To have endured this and yet to have remained decent in the process, aside from those exceptions of human weakness – that is what has steeled and hardened us. This is an unwritten, and a never to be written page of glory in our history. Because we know how difficult the situation for us would be today if in that city – given all the air raids, the burdens and deprivations of the war – we were still saddled with the Jews: as secret saboteurs, agitators and rabble-rousers. By now, we would probably be back facing a situation similar to that of 1916/1917 – if the Jews were still lodged within the body of the German people. We took from them the assets and riches they possessed. We had the moral right, we had the duty toward our own Volk, to destroy that people which wished to destroy us. In general, however, we can say that – out of a feeling of love for our people – we have fulfilled this most arduous of tasks. And that we have suffered no damage or harm as a result – in our inner being, our souls, our character.

Secret Police – Terror Specialists

The police frequently worked in conjunction with the *Sicherheitsdienst* or SS security forces, the intelligence service of the SS. Created in 1932 by Reinhard Heydrich, the SD was the first Nazi Party intelligence organisation to be established and was considered a 'sister organisation' to the Gestapo. On 9 June 1934, it became the sole 'Party information service,' then in 1938 was ordained as the intelligence organisation for the state as well as for the Party, supporting the Gestapo and working with the General and Interior Administration.

The SD was tasked with the detection of actual or potential enemies of the Nazi leadership and the neutralisation of this opposition. To fulfil this task, the SD created an organisation of agents and informants throughout the Reich and later throughout the occupied territories. The organisation consisted of a few hundred full-time agents and several thousand informants. The SD was the information-gathering agency while the Gestapo, and to a degree the *Kriminalpolizei*, functioned as the executive agency of the political police system. Both the SD and the Gestapo were effectively under the control of Heinrich Himmler as Chief of the German Police.

The SD provided the main source of security force personnel in occupied territories, its battalions typically placed under the command of the SS and Police Leaders. It members also maintained a presence at all concentration camps and supplied its members as needed to such special organisations as the *Einsatzgruppen* mobile execution units. The SD was also the primary agency, in conjunction with the *Ordnungspolizei*, assigned to maintain order and security in the Jewish ghettos of Poland. Much of the killing in the ghettos can be attributed to SD troops under the command of local SS and Police Leaders.

Special Action Killers – Face to Face Mass Murder

Formed in anticipation of the invasion of the Soviet Union, the initial four SS *Einsatzgruppen* (designated A, B, C, D) consisted of between 195 and 900 volunteer members as well as an additional 3 to 4,000 men from the Criminal Police, Gestapo and Waffen-SS, as well as Reserve Police Battalion 9. A fifth was formed in June 1941 'for special tasks', operating behind Group B in the Ukraine and Belorussia. As the mass killings progressed, various police battalions were assigned to assist the *Einsatzgruppen*.

Each of the original four *Einsatzgruppen* was designated an area of operation:

Einsatzgruppe A: Baltic nations of Latvia, Lithuania and Estonia
Einsatzgruppe B: Eastern Poland and Belorussia
Einsatzgruppe C: Western Ukraine
Einsatzgruppe D: Southern Ukraine and Crimea

By the spring of 1943, the relatively small number of individuals comprising the *Einsatzgruppen* and Order Police Battalions (PB) mobile killing teams had accounted for an estimated 1,500,000 murdered Jews and thousands of gypsies, Soviet commissars, partisans and other enemies of the Third Reich in Eastern Europe and Russia.

For example, *Einsatzgruppen* A was composed of approximately 1,000 men from the Gestapo and Criminal Police, the *Sicherheitsdienst* (SD), the Uniformed Police and the Waffen-SS. By 31 January 1942, *Einsatzgruppe* A, the largest of the four specialised killing units, reported a tally of 229,052 Jews (men, women and children) killed. Of the unit's total staff, only half were 'hands-on' executioners, with the rest providing support as drivers, cooks, clerks, etc. Calculations therefore estimate each executioner had individually murdered over 500 people, with more victims to come.

Further calculations of 'efficiency' can be applied to members of the *Sonderkommando* 11a of *Einsatzgruppen* D. During an *aktion* taking place in the Jewish ghetto in Nikolayev during three days in September 1941, the four teams of ten men, each firing every ten minutes for six hours (with a two-hour lunch break), shot some 5,000 Jews.

Seeking means to transport victims to shooting sites, special execution vans were designed and built, camouflaged with painted windows and decorations, into which the unsuspecting were thrown. For example, *Einsatzkommando* 10A of Group D operating during June 1942 in the northern Caucasus called up one of the 10-ton vehicles, which the local Russians called the 'the soul catchers'. The van was sent to a home for 270 physically and mentally handicapped children, with repeated trips made under the guise of 'outings'. Some of the children were required to step in and out of their graves to see if it 'fit'. Eventually the vans were fitted out as mobile gas chambers.

Serving the Bottomless Pits

When encountering large numbers of victims, the killers developed techniques to improve efficiency. If a child had difficulty walking, they would sometimes be carried in the arms of their parent or sometimes even in the arms of their killers. Later, to conserve ammunition, the smaller children and infants were clubbed to death with rifle butts or truncheons, bayoneted or simply tossed alive into the mass graves to be smothered to death, again sometimes in the arms of their parents. Often the non-Jewish villagers would observe the mass graves heaving and groaning for days as the bloated and decaying bodies of the dead released gases.

The mass shootings, though relatively 'crude' when compared to establishment of the processing technology of the Extermination Camps, were part and parcel of the so-called 'Final Solution to the Jewish Question,' one for which the Nazi mindset had only one answer: the annihilation of all of European Jewry, some 11,000,00 in total.

The killers conducted their *aktions* with ruthless, seemingly impossible efficiency. In the case of the Babi Yar massacre that took place in the Ukrainian city of Kiev during just two days, 28–29 September 1941, some 34,000 Russian Jewish men, women and children were shot to death by a few handfuls of Germans, including members of Police Battalions 45, 303 and 314, with the corpses being buried in a trench 60 yards long and 8 feet deep. Later the Germans ordered Jewish slave labourers to dig up the bones and grind them to dust in an attempt to hide their crime, then the workers were themselves killed.

A well planned-out subterfuge was the main German weapon that included promises of work, of remaining with their families, of food. Moreover the victims could not fathom they were being led to their deaths. Even the Germans were amazed at how easily their victims seemingly acquiesced to the procedure, deriding them as 'like sheep to the slaughter'.

Often the victims were forced to walk long distances to the execution sites to weaken them and lessen any resistance, with them then being forced to lie in the hot summer sun for hours without water to further debilitate them. Then they were made to wait hours for their turn as the mass graves were filled, watching others be killed before their eyes.

The killers worried little about escape attempts as they counted on the fact that mothers and fathers would be unable to abandon their children and elderly grandparents. In addition, they knew the Jews had nowhere to escape to for in most cases their fellow non-Jewish countrymen either shunned them for fear of reprisals by the Germans or in many cases collaborated with the killers in the operations, often for reward or to claim their homes and property.

Techniques for killing varied. In the early days of the mass shootings, the male prisoners were shot first, followed by the women and children. Then it was thought better to mix in the women and children rather than leave them for the last, since a concentration of wailing women and children placed more strain on the killers, who often returned splattered with blood and brain matter. Machine guns were employed for more efficient 'special handling' of large numbers of victims. Often joining the special SS *Einsatzgruppen* killing squads, along with members of the Police Battalions, were Waffen-SS troops and regular German Army soldiers, and on occasion members of the Luftwaffe and *Kriegsmarine* ground forces too.

Some members of the killing teams considered the solo pistol execution method too 'Bolshevik' in nature so opted for a longer shooting range with a twenty-man team facing the victims lined up before a previously excavated ditch. The method involved a pair of policemen targeting one victim, therefore totalling eight to ten shot in one volley. This long-range approach sometimes proved fatal for the killers themselves since the 'Hiwis', or the volunteer non-German helpers recruited from local inhabitants, were often so drunk that because of their shaky aim occasionally wounded or killed their German overseers or fellow executioners.

Regarding accessories to murder, several Eastern European and Baltic countries provided indigenous and often enthusiastic volunteers. For example, Lithuanian *Schutzmannshaft* members murdered 78,000 Jewish men, women and children during *aktions* in Lithuania and in Belarus. Romania was only second to Germany for the number of Jews killed by its military and civilians. Ukrainians often served alongside the mobile killing units and as concentration and death camp guards.

Post-war only seven of the *Einsatzkommando* officers were executed for their crimes, with another seventy-one being given sentences from life to less than five years, those sentences often reduced. In the midst of the Cold War neither the German government nor the American authorities were prone to exert effort in seeking further prosecutions. Most of the mass murderers died in their beds of old age in Germany.

It was often literally overnight that civilian police units were transported from cities like Hamburg and Vienna to conquered territory in Eastern Europe, where they became the vanguard in the extermination of the Jewish populations. Their duties could also include combating partisans, or 'bandits' as Nazi terminology referred to them, a catch-all term that allowed for treating partisans outside the pale of the Geneva Conference rules, in effect 'legalising' wholesale murder.

The question of how seemingly 'ordinary men,' family men, with their own wives and children, could murder thousands of women and children, even infants is often raised. The matter is compounded by the fact that most of the policemen were not fanatical Nazis, rather civilian policemen suddenly transferred from their metropolitan homes and jobs to the hinterlands of Poland and Russia.

A very partial listing of the Police Battalions (PB) and examples of their actions includes:

PB   1 – Included one rifle regiment and two Ukrainian *Schutzmannshaft* – operated in Poland and the Ukraine

PB   2 – Faced Red Army counteroffensive, remnants later posted to Holland

PB   6 – Joined Security Division, decimated in 1944 by Russian forces

PB   9 – Joined three separate *Einsatzgruppen* including C and D; documented murder of 52,000 by December 1941.

PB 11 – *Einsatzgruppen* attachment, actions at Kovno Ghetto

PB 21 – Composed of one rifle regiment and two Ukrainian *Schutzmannshaft*, crushed rebellion at Bialystok Ghetto, then saw late war action in Warsaw against Red forces

PB 22 – *Einsatzgruppen* actions including Riga, Latvia

PB 24 – *Aktions* around Kiev, later decimated by Soviet forces in 1944

PB 32 – *Einsatzgruppen* actions including Lvov 1941

PB 45 – *Einsatzgruppen* actions including Babi Yar mass murder, later posted to Slovenia

PB 61 – Warsaw Ghetto guards

PB 67 – *Einsatzgruppen* actions include Zamosc (Ghetto 'cleared') and Bigoraj (centre of Polish Home Army resistance)

PB 101 – 500 men responsible for at least 83,000 murders (documented in milestone book *Ordinary Men*)

PB 303 – *Einsatzgruppen* actions including Zhitomir and Bar Yar mass murders

PB 309 – The 1st and 3rd Company joined the 221st Security Division in burning alive some 700 Jews inside a synagogue in the Polish city of Bialystok; also joined *Einsatzkommando* 8. Thousands more murdered.

PB 314 – *Einsatzgruppen* actions including those in Vinnitsa area where in total some 200,000 Jews were killed

PB 315 – Formed in Berlin as Police Regiment 11 took part in a twelve-day rampage through several southern Russian towns, killing the inhabitants often by burning, including the children.

Contained within the following pages are exceptionally rare photographs and documents relating to one of the many police execution units, in this case the Order Police Battalion 322. Originally formed in Vienna as a training battalion, PB 322 would operate in various occupied territories including Holland, Poland and Russia. On 9 June 1941 they were transported to Warsaw, where they joined Police Regiment *Mitte* (Centre), one of the three Order Police regiments later sent to Russia after its invasion on 22 June of that year. Another group was formed in Belgrade, Serbia, in July 1942, composed of ethnic German Serbs.

Attached to an *Einsatzgruppen* execution team, PB 322 took part in actions in Bialystok during August 1941, Mogilev in October 1941 and Minsk from November 1941 into July 1942. They also carried out executions in Serbia and Croatia, the latter in the late stages of the war during 1944–45.

PB 322 consisted of three companies each composed of 150 men as well as some forty transport personnel and thirty headquarters office staff. Working in Russia as part of Police Regiment Centre, they followed in the wake of the regular army sweeping through the area. According to post-war testimony, their initial duties were safeguarding railways and other installations, traffic control and enforcing law and order in the rear guard area. They went on to battle partisans and execute Soviet officials found among POWs, sometimes dying in battle themselves when encountering armed resisters and Red Army troops.

Members of PB 322 also found themselves engaged in a bizarre experiment conducted by the SS: the establishment of a special forest enclave in which Nazi scientists planned to replicate through genetic engineering long-extinct animals linked to ancient Germany, the creatures including massive oxen known as aurochs, the ancestor of modern domestic cattle. Under the orders of *Reichsmarshall* Hermann Göring, also Germany's Master of the Hunt, the area selected for the natural game preserve was a 580-square-mile primeval forest in eastern Poland, the area known as Białowieża and the last refuge for some of Europe's rarest animals including bison, moose, wild horses and wolves. Toward that goal, in July 1941, shortly after the invasion of the Soviet Union by Germany, PB 322 was sent in to 'cleanse' the area of all human inhabitants, especially the Jewish settlements, either by deportation or outright mass murder. In the seven days between 25 July and 1 August 1941, 183 families of the small village of Budaya were eliminated. Within three years, some 20,000 would be expelled including Poles and Byelorussians, while the entire Jewish population was eradicated, the latter never to return. The Białowieża Forest became the scene of some of the first mass execution of Jews by the German police and their accomplices, and as such is considered the initial staging ground for the Final Solution.

Reportedly PB 322's commanding officer and his adjutant initially objected to his men being ordered to participate in the shooting of Jews. Eventually the adjutant was able to have himself transferred to a training unit and avoided taking part in the murders, which had apparently appalled him. Members of police and other execution squads were given the option of not participating in the shootings without fear of punishment, and a few did abstain, but in general there was an overabundance of volunteers – especially after the participating individuals became inured to the slaughter. The meticulous documentation by the Germans themselves accounted for every last murder, the statistics broken down into men, women and children, as so providing ample evidence of their crimes.

PB 322's complicity in the racial war increased during the *aktions* that took place in Minsk and later in Mogilev. One of its officers testified in a 1965 German court that he tried to conduct the executions in 'a disciplined and efficient manner without unnecessary suffering'. He went on to say that he made sure the victims were dead and covered with dirt before the next victims were brought forth. He also testified that he ordered the trucks delivering the Jews not to park too close to the execution pits in order to spare them the sight of their fellows being killed. He and another fellow officer were found not guilty by a Freiburg court in a decision that stated 'they had themselves being confronted with the danger of being executed if they had disobeyed orders'. The German judges decided that there was no other option but obedience – a rather hollow echo of the much heard argument 'I was only following orders'. Subsequent research has shown no member of a killing group was ever severely punished for opting not to participate in an execution. In fact, cases arose where members of police units challenged SS *Einsatzgruppe*n orders for the killing of Jews without any repercussions against those who refused to take part in massacres.

Of the death they left in their own wake, the official PB 322 logbook notations included the terse notations:

August 18, 1941 – 4.00 Jewish action in Narweka-Mala. 259 women and 162 children transported by lorry to Kobryn. 282 Jews were shot.
Bialystok: July 12–13, 1941 – 3,000 Jews shot
Mogilev: October 19, 1941 – 3,700 Jews shot
Minsk: November 1941 – 19,000 Jews shot
Minsk: July 28–30, 1942 – 9,000 Jews shot

An excerpt from a letter posted 5 October 1941 by SS and Police Lieutenant Walter Mattner, a member of the staff of the Higher SS and Police Leader's 'Central Russia,' to his wife reads:

... I must tell you something else. I took part in a mass killing the day before yesterday. When we shot the Jews brought by the first truck my hand trembled somewhat during the shooting, but one gets used to it. By the tenth truck I was already aiming steadily and shooting accurately at the many women, children, and babies. I thought about the two infants that I have at home, to whom this gang would do exactly the same, if not ten times worse. The death we were according them was a short and beautiful one compared to the hellish sufferings of the many thousands in the torture chambers of the Soviet GPU. The babies went flying through the air in a big arc and we shot them down as they flew, before they fell into the grave or into the water. Let's get rid of this brood of Jews, who pushed all of Europe into war and is now agitating America also until it too is dragged into the war.

Walking Among the Brambles
Occasionally policemen's wives and girlfriends would
visit them in the field, where they could be invited to
witness mass executions as a form of excursion.

Police Post-Mortem – Complicity Compounded

The secretly recorded conversations of ordinary German soldiers, airmen and naval personnel held in a British POW facility were published in English in 2012, the bestselling book first published in German in 2011 by historian Sonke Neitzel after discovering the documents in the National Archives in the city of Kew. Titled *Soldiers: Diaries of Fighting, Killing and Dying*, the book exposes the widespread knowledge of genocide, and in fact its enthusiastic support by the German Army rather than solely by SS 'fanatics'. The following excerpt concerns the matter of what was termed 'execution tourism':

> The splendidly named General Edwin Graf von Rothkirch und Trach explained to a fellow inmate: 'I knew an SS leader in Kutno, Poland, and we chatted about this and that and he said; "God, when you want to film something, why didn't you say so? I mean, timewise, it doesn't matter. We shoot them in the mornings, but if that is inconvenient, we have others that we can always shoot in the afternoon."'
>
> Lieutenant Mueller-Riezenburg, in a transcript made on Christmas Day 1943, said: 'The SS invited us over for a Jew-shoot. The whole troop went off with their weapons and joined in. Everyone was allowed to pick which one they wanted to shoot.'

Justice Abridged and Humanity Violated

'A man is the lord over life and death when he gets an order to shoot 300 children and he kills 150 himself.'

Captain Lothar Heimbach, member of *Einsatzgruppen D*,
a documented killing team responsible for 91,728 victims.
(Lothar was never brought to trial for his crimes.)

The Cold War found the Allies, including the Americans, more interested in benefiting from the killers' study of the Soviets and as a result incorporated many Nazis into their intelligence organisations. The post-war German so-called 'de-Nazified' government was in reality populated by many ex-members of the SS, while the *polizei*, including war criminals, returned home to resume their security roles. In so doing, they were able to conceal their crimes and offer protection to their fellow war criminals. For example, in 1965 former SS *Sturmbahnführer* Eric Hassche was found employed in police service in Darmstadt while Kurt Huhn, previously a company commander in the SS Police, was ensconced as a police group commander in the US sector in West Berlin. Hubert Marbach, ex-company commander of an SD-*Einsatzgruppen* killing team, was discovered acting as the director of a police school in Bonn. Joining him in that city, the capital of West Germany, was Paulus Meier, a mass-murder battalion commander of the SS and police. Another *Einsatzkommander*, Karl Potke, was found holding the position of director of police in Hamburg. Many others held similar police positions of authority across West Germany, twenty years after their victims had been sent to their mass graves.

Not until May 2006 did the German government release some 16 miles of Third Reich documents that had 'for reasons of privacy' been withheld from researchers. More than sixty years had passed – time enough for any implicated in the documents of Nazi era crimes to have escaped justice. One result of the disclosure of the documents revealed that that the network of concentration camps, ghettos and labour camps was nearly three times more extensive than previously thought, with some 20,000 camps and ghettos identified.

Of the thousands who took part in the mass murders of over 1 million Jewish men, women and children by the SS, police and *Einsatzgruppe* killing teams and their Wehrmacht and foreign helpers, the post-war German judicial system investigated some 1,700 killing squad members, of which 136 were brought to trial. Of that number fifty-three sentences were handed out between 1950 and 1991. Eight of the convicted received life sentences, the others prison terms ranging from two to four years. Many of the sentences were later shortened or commuted. In summary, post-war German 'reluctance' to prosecute its past resulted in few convictions and then those generally followed by reduction in sentencing despite the fact few if any of the convicted ever expressed any remorse.

The Short List

Group Leader Otto Ohlendorf:	Death sentence (executed on 8 June 1951)
Heinz Jost:	Life imprisonment
Erich Naumann:	Death sentence (executed on 8 June 1951)
Dr Otto Rasch:	Released from adjudication due to illness
Erwin Schulz:	Twenty years imprisonment
Walter Blume:	Death sentence (commuted to life imprisonment)
Dr Franz Six:	Twenty years imprisonment
Paul Blobel:	Death sentence (executed on 7 June 1951)
Lothar Fendler:	Ten years imprisonment
Eugen Steimle:	Death sentence (commuted to life imprisonment)
Ernst Biberstein:	Death sentence (commuted to life imprisonment)
Willy Seibert:	Death sentence (commuted to fifteen years imprisonment)
Gustav Nosske:	Life imprisonment

Adolf Ott:	Death sentence (commuted to life imprisonment, he later escaped, never to be recaptured)
Waldemar Klingelhöfer:	Death sentence (commuted to fifteen years imprisonment)
Dr Eduard Strauch:	Death sentence (commuted due to illness)
Mattias Graf:	Fifteen years imprisonment
Dr Werner Braune:	Death sentence (executed on 7 June 1951)
Walter Hänsch:	Death sentence (commuted to fifteen years imprisonment)
Martin Sandberger:	Death sentence (commuted to life imprisonment)
Waldemar von Radetzsky:	Twenty years imprisonment
Felix Rühl:	Ten years imprisonment
Heinz Schübert:	Death sentence (commuted to life imprisonment)
Emil Hausmann:	Committed suicide on 31 July 1947

Twenty-four ex-SS officials were convicted in Case No. 9 (the so-called *Einsatzgruppen* Trial), held by the International Military Tribunal at Nuremberg from 27 September 1947 to 9 April 1948. While fourteen were sentenced to death, only four were executed; twelve had their executions commuted, one person committed suicide during the trial and the remainder were sentenced to various terms of imprisonment.

Untold unmarked graves, both large and small, lay scattered across the vastness of Eastern Europe and Ukraine, some found, many still lost. The incidents of brutal murder are legion. The following is but one example.

The Massacre of the Children of Beylaya Tserkov, Ukraine – 20 August 1941

In 1973 West German courts tried Lt August Hafner of *Sonderkommando* 4a. During the trial, Hafner stated that his commander, Paul Blobel, had ordered him to have a group of nineteen children executed, their parents already having been murdered. Said Hafner:

I asked him, 'By whom should the shooting be carried out?' He answered, 'By the Waffen-SS.' I raised an objection and said, 'They are all young men. How are we going to answer them if we make them shoot small children?'

To this he said, 'Then use your men.' I then said, 'How can they do that? They have small children as we.' This tug-of-war lasted about ten minutes. I suggested that the Ukrainian militia of the *Feldkommandant* should shoot the children. There were no objections from either side to the suggestion.

I went to the woods alone. The Wehrmacht had already dug a grave. The children were brought along in a tractor. I had nothing to do with the technical procedure. The Ukrainians were standing around trembling.

The children were taken down from the tractor. They were lined up along the top of the grave and shot so that they fell into it. The Ukrainians did not aim at any particular part of the body. They fell into the grave. The wailing was indescribable. I shall never forget the scene throughout my life. I find it very hard to bear.

I particularly remember a small fair-haired girl who took me by the hand. She too was shot later. Many children were hit four or five times before they died.

Sonderkommando 4a was disbanded in 1943 after murdering 59,018 people. Hafner received an eight-year sentence.

In October 2014, an announcement was made by the Los Angeles-based Simon Wiesenthal Centre that it had identified seventy-six men and four women who served in the *Einsatzgruppen* and who may have been still living. The names were gleaned from a list of some 1,100 from the estimated 3,000 members of the death squads. Efforts were made to produce an investigation by German authorities with the warning that time was literally running out to bring them to justice because of their advanced ages.

Pre-Third Reich Roots –
The Men in the Shako Helmets

Above left: **Police Forces on Parade – To Protect and Serve**
In a post-First World War 1920s scene, civilian police march through the streets. Often well armed, they were employed by the Weimar authorities to deal with the street demonstrations and various political intrigues that often resorted to gunfire. Policemen were often the target for assassination by both communist and ultra-nationalist factions, including the nascent Nazi Party.

Above right: **State-of-the-Art Mobile Communications, 1925**
Two policemen pose with the latest wireless transceiver equipment, including a massive tube radio with its antenna and rear-facing 'horn' speaker.

Above left: 'In Remembrance of our Wedding', 18 June 1927

A civilian policeman clutching his ceremonial sword stands with his beautifully gowned bride holding a bouquet of roses. He stares skyward as she gazes into the camera. On this date in Germany, the Nazi Party along with the SA 'Brownshirts' and fledging SS were growing in strength and popularity. In the following August, upon the occasion of the Third Party Day rally held in Nuremburg, Hitler would make his public declaration, marrying *Weltanschauung*, his obsessive 'World View' ideology, with *Lebensraum*, or the need for increased 'living space'. He also listed his perceived mortal enemies of Germany – democracy, internationalism and pacifism – before further linking all three as a creation of the Jews. A hint of things to come, a state policy of annihilation would also harness elements of the German police to the task.

Above right: Formal Studio Portrait, 1920

While her husband wears his traditional *Tschako* (shako) cap, she wears the latest fashion in women's hats. Both hold gloves in opposite hands to help 'balance' out the composition.

Prisoner
A German civilian policeman poses with a young girl in handcuffs, her crimes unknown. A number of larger German cities produced so-called youth gangs that disturbed German society with their wild clothes and 'anti-social' behaviour including dancing to American jazz and engaging in 'free sex' as well as harassing Hitler Youth members and occasionally petty theft and vandalism. The Gestapo would send many to concentration camps.

Early Nazi Supporter Arrested, 1920s
An official Party photograph spotlights the defiance of a member of the Nazi Party, demonstrating his allegiance despite being under police arrest. Captioning on the reverse of the image states his name as Felix Albrecht. Research indicates he joined the Party in 1927. A professional artist, he would go on to design propaganda posters, joining the SS in 1933 and later becoming a Third Reich film censor, then Chief of Public Welfare of the Nazi Party in 1938. As an SS-*Obersturmführer* (Senior Assault Leader), his drawings appeared in the early Third Reich book *Deutschland Erwacht* (*Germany Awake*). He was also the author of *Germany's Great Leader* and was later promoted to SS Captain in the Waffen-SS, serving as a recruiter.

Munster: Weimar Republic Era, 1925
A group of Weimar Republic shako-helmeted policemen, rifles at the ready, pose for a group photo that was converted into a postcard. While most have adopted a stern expression, several apparently take the occasion less seriously when facing a camera.
The city's leading Catholic cleric would become a vocal anti-Nazi, which brought him repercussions. (Original photo postcard processed by Sonntags Foto-Hause of Westphalia)

Mass Swearing-In Portrait of 1st Battalion, 22 September 1925
At this pivotal point Hitler has been released from Landsburg Prison after his confinement following the failed 'Beer Hall Putsch' plot to seize control of the government. He re-established the Nazi Party in February, followed in April with the birth of the SS, with Himmler assuming its leadership role.

Above left: Non-Uniform Uniformity
A wide variety of facial types and expressions populate the portrait.

Above right: 'Traffic Control Policeman' – Composite Figures Produced as Donation Gifts from the Winter Relief Fund (WHW)
The 2-inch-tall toys were among several hundred various figures handed out as gifts to those donating to the annual Winter Relief drives (*Winterhilfswerk*, aka WHW) conducted by the National Socialist People's Welfare Organisation (*Nationalsozialistische Volkswohlfahrt*). First introduced in 1931 with the slogan 'None shall starve nor freeze,' the collection efforts continued throughout the war years, specifically in the months of October through March for the benefit of those Germans in need of food, clothing, coal and later war damage relief.

Berlin: Model City Policemen – Traffic Control Strategy, 28 February 1928
Local Weimar Republic police officials discuss a course of action to deal with the city's increasing traffic congestion. Towering over a meticulously crafted model of the city, one policeman points out a traffic island where officers would direct the flow of vehicles. The image is evocative of the Nazi Secret Police State that would take godlike control of all avenues of German life five years in the future, including the policemen themselves.

While Josef Goebbels had actually called for Hitler's banishment from the early Nazi Party, he was eventually won over, and by January 1928 Hitler, recognizing his talents, placed Goebbels in charge of the state propaganda apparatus, which would eventually monopolise all media toward its political, ideological and military ends.

27. Jan. 1930.

Lunch Break, New Year 1930

A photo postcard features a mix of young *Reichswehr* police recruits, their officers and a single civilian providing the camera with his profile in his Hamburg hat. The date of the photo places the moment thirteen days prior to an historic event in the Nazi mytho-history. On 14 January 1930, an SA troop leader named Horst Wessel was allegedly killed by communists. Goebbels anointed him to Nazi sainthood, with him being further lauded by the song 'Horst Wessel' launched as the official Nazi Party anthem. While Wessel had previously penned the lyrics, the music chosen was reportedly a Salvation Army tune. The actual facts suggest that Wessel was a pimp for prostitutes and was killed in a brawl over a girl.

Rifle Range

Policemen take turns firing from the prone position. During the turbulent 1920s Weimar days of violent political demonstrations involving factions of the right and left as well as anarchist groups, the police often fought pitched street battles and as a result were equipped with military-grade weapons, including machine guns and flamethrowers.

Policemen and Police Dogs

A bicycle-mounted patrolman poses with two leashed canine comrades. He wears a First World War-era Iron Cross on his tunic, as well as the traditional shako helmet.

Timely Congratulations
Two policemen pose for their portrait during a celebration of their 25th anniversary in uniform. Along with bouquets of flowers and various potted plants decorating the table are gifts in appreciation of their service. One has received a pocket watch, the other a clock.

Above left: **Medals of Service**
A member of the *Gendamerie* wears two long-service medals, apparently the four- and twelve-year awards, indicating service that began pre-Second World War.

Above right: **Police Raid Communist Party Offices, 1933**
In an official press photo civilian police are shown sifting through documents found at the commemoratively named Karl-Liebknect House in Berlin on 24 February 1933. A month earlier Hitler had assumed power, then immediately began striking out at any adversaries, the communists high on the list. Karl Liebkneckt had been a co-leader along with Rosa Luxembourg of the Spartacists, a group of radical socialists who founded the German Communist Party. In January 1919 after mounting a failed revolution against the Weimar government, the pair was arrested and summarily executed. By 1928 the Spartacists, though a minority, held more Reichstag seats than the Nazi Party, but as Hitler gained total power the German Communist Party soon ceased to exist.

***Above left*: Police Service Publication, December 1936**
A photo montage spotlights the *Ordnungspolizei* (Order Police) technical school and its various departments, including communications, motor pool and armoury. Images include BMW and NSU motorcycles and the police riding them on patrol. The Order Police would eventually number 300,000 members.

***Above right*: Take Your Chances**
Policemen have convinced a woman, hammer in hand, to play their game of chance, her money going to the Winter Relief Drive. Visible beneath the gaming table is the ubiquitous swastika. In the background a member of the Hitler Youth watches the game in play, their members very active as WHW donation collectors. As indicated by the name of the coin slotted box on the table, *Zaubergroschen* (or 'magic dime'), the game may involve hammering in small metal pieces into a board, thus creating a design of some kind ... after making a donation.

Winter Relief Fund Drive – Donation Gift
The figure of a *polizei* on horseback in formal uniform could stand alone or via a string attached to a coat or shirt button. Much pressure was applied on everyone to contribute to the WHW in some form. Those who shirked were listed as slackers in the newspapers, sometimes even being physically attacked. The collectible 'tinnies' were made of wood, glass, paper, terracotta, metal and plastic, and were produced in some 8,000 different designs including a wide variety of birds and insects, nursery rhyme and fairy-tale characters, as well as historical personages including Adolf Hitler.

Collecting for the Winter Relief Drive

A large and imposing police officer 'accepts' donations from civilians who have gathered at a street fair complete with carnival games, including a shooting gallery in the background. Dangling from the policeman's tunic are three of the white toy horse donation trinkets.

Collision

Policemen wearing motorcycle helmets investigate a traffic accident, the unhappy drivers standing nearby. The officer in the foreground carries a measuring tape. Both wear the distinctive dark cuffs of the Nazi-era militarised *polizei*.

Crowd Control

Civilian police, with help from a member of the SA, hold back a rapturous crowd waiting to catch a glimpse of their new leader.

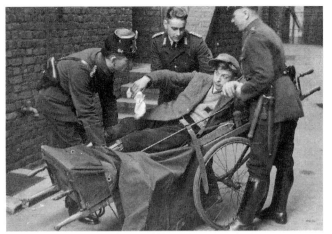

To Protect and Serve
Civilian policemen are photographed for the media as they come to the aid of a handicapped boy. Later Nazi programs to eliminate the mentally and physically disabled resulted in the murder of over 200,000, with elements of the police taking part in their round-up and transport to the euthanasia centres.

Nazi Boycott of Jewish Businesses
Civilian Police and Gestapo inspect papers of Jewish men detained during a nationwide boycott targeting Jewish businesses. Implemented by Josef Goebbels, the boycott began on the Saturday morning of 1 April 1933 at 10 a.m. In reality, most German civilians ignored the boycott effort; plus, since it was the Jewish Sabbath, many smaller Jewish shops were already closed for the day.

However, the event was a tipping point that saw a swift devolution into anti-Jewish laws and measures. Eventually, over 400 such laws were imposed that increasingly tightened the noose first for German Jews, then for those caught within occupied territories as German aggression spread across Europe.

Flame Proof Composite
Joining a contingent of firemen with their distinctive helmets are policemen wearing their civilian shako headgear.

Polizei Veterans
A dramatic range of faces stare out from a group portrait of rural (*Gendarmerie*) and (*Feurpolizei*) fire police, several of whom perhaps served in the First World War.

Above left: Fire Protection Policeman's Family Portrait

Above right: Fire Police with Fawn
The two men flanking the deer wear uniform shoulder boards indicating the high rank of *Meister*, or leader. Subjected to ever-increasing Allied aerial bombing often resulting in firestorms, the fire police, aided by volunteers, often faced catastrophic conditions yet continued to perform their duties in the rescue of endangered civilians, often with their own lives in great peril.

Munster, Hamm or Gelsenkirchen: Field Police Gathering
This photo was taken somewhere in the heavily industrialised Ruhr Valley. Several of the civilians wear
Nazi Party pins while others show the effect of the beer. An oil refining centre, Munster, located in North
Rhine-Westphalia, suffered 63 per cent total destruction from Allied bombing, being targeted also because
of its large Wehrmacht troop garrison and the location of a military command centre. Much of the
militarisation of the city resulted as a counter-response to the early anti-Nazi stance taken by the Bishop
of Munster, Cardinal Clemens von Galen, who although an opponent of democracy and an advocate of the
war against Communist Russia, expressed strong opposition to the euthanasia program and racist policies.

Above left: **Half-Full**
The adjacent city of Hamm, a coal-mining and railway hub, was also extensively destroyed by Allied
bombing. As for the nearby town of Gelsenkirhen, it was for a time the most important coal-mining centre in
Europe. During the Second World War it was also a major oil refining area and the target of Allied bombing
that resulted in three-quarters of its destruction. During the Kristallnacht riots staged across Germany on
9 November 1938, the city's Jewish businesses, homes, synagogue and cemetery were attacked by the local
inhabitants. It was also the location of a subcamp of Buchenwald holding some 2,000 Hungarian women
slave labourers. As Nazi policy forbade any prisoners from seeking shelter during an air raid, many died
during the Allied bombing raids.

Above right: **And All Ages**
Many older men in police uniform guarded buildings, checked border areas, collected custom taxes, watched
for poachers and issued traffic tickets.

Police Pantheon

Wearing various Third Reich uniforms as well as civilian attire, a group of city officials and police officers pose for a group portrait on the steps of an unidentified government building. The caps of the policemen show the late pattern emblem while the two central figures wearing ceremonial daggers appear to be members of the *Reichsluftschutzbund* (RLB), the organisation formed on 28 April 1933 and charged with educating the civilian public regarding all matters relating to civil defence, and who, as a result, liaised with the civilian police. Several of the civilians wear Nazi Party pins.

Above left: **Breslau: Mounted Shako Helmeted Police, 1930**
Postmarked 13 September 1930 and addressed to a Paul Vogl, this photo postcard was produced at the Paul Weich workshop, specialists in photographing horse riding and racing as well as carriage driving. The quartet of horses appear to be the much-prized thoroughbred Trakehner breed.

Located in the Silesian Lowlands on the River Order, Breslau was an important city that over the centuries variously found itself under the flags of Poland, Bohemia, Hungary, the Austrian Empire and lastly Germany, becoming the largest city east of Berlin during the Nazi era. While it was historically considered a liberal left wing bastion, as it grew strongly pro-Nazi attacks by the local police began against Polish institutions, and several concentration and slave labour camps were established in the area.

Above right: **Breslau: Escape and No Escape, 1931**
During a competition in August 1931, a police horseman clears an obstacle under the observant eye of another policeman/event official, with spectators visible in the distant background. It would be two years before Hitler and the Nazi Party would take over the reins of the police horse traning; however, anti-Semitic riots had broken out in Breslau during 1923 as the early Nazi movement spread. In late 1938 Jewish synagogues, schools and cemeteries were destroyed and all cultural activities were banned. Deportations began in 1941, the trains taking the Jewish ex-citizens to their deaths at Auschwitz, Treblinka, Sobibor and other extermination camps. Most of the city's 10,000 Jewish residents perished.

Frankfurt: Police in Costume, 1939
Members of the Frankfurt city police appear as bearded conquistadors sometime in July 1939 during one of the annual historical festivals. With the rise to power of Hitler, military personnel were often called upon to take part as 'extras' in Goebbels' street pageants and historical film epics, some 2,000 motion pictures being produced by the Nazi Ministry of Propaganda and Entertainment. In this month Nazi Foreign Minister von Ribbentrop travels to Moscow for talks with his Russian counterparts, presaging the infamous Soviet-German Non-Aggression Pact, aka the Molotov-Ribbentrop Pact, which will allow for their mutual invasion of Poland in the upcoming September.

Berlin *Wacht* Parade: Wehrmacht Honour Guard
As if echoing the chariot sculpture surmounting Berlin's famed Brandenburg Gate, visible in the background, a pair of white police horses shares the road with a motorcyclist and a military band. The photograph was reproduced by the Nazi propaganda machine and sold commercially to the German public.

Transition – Serving the Swastika

Metamorphosis on Parade
Civilian police still don their traditional shako helmets but wear the uniforms of the Third Reich's Wehrmacht. More troops are visible in the background as spectators line the city streets of Berlin for what may be the annual 'Day of the Police' celebration.

Exchange of Headgear
The Third Reich's new police identification included insignia found on their caps and echoed on the left sleeve of their tunics. Their dark brown cuffs and grey-green uniforms would later cause them to be referred to as 'Hitler's Green Army'. The transition of the civilian policeman into a political policeman brought more than a change in uniform and the loss of the distinctively shaped civilian helmet.

Above left: Medals Past and Present
A veteran policeman poses with First World War awards, including a Wound Badge and Iron Cross First Class, as well as more current Third Reich long service honours.

Above right: Transition of Uniform and Mind-set
The early transitional uniform of the *Gendarmerie* shows leather strapping, which would be discontinued. He wears the newly instigated militarised police cap insignia, although not yet the new Wehrmacht uniform tunic.

Black Leather Jackets and Motorised Police
The license plate on the large delivery truck indicates the location is somewhere in Westphalia, the inn's name indicating Munich. Members of the *Nationalsozialistisches Kraftfahrkorps* (NSKK) were initially tasked with the operation of high performance vehicles and as chauffeurs for party members, but were then redirected to serve in the German military transport corps when war called for their skills, which were substantial since horses had made up the prime moving forces of German troops. A paramilitary organisation themselves, some NSKK joined Waffen-SS and police units in conducting arrests, brutal interrogations and, in some cases, mass executions.

Above left: **Mirror Images**
Two young pre-war policemen pose for the camera, one holding black gloves, the other, white.

Above right: **Proud Hunters**
Three rural policemen, one still wearing the traditional shako cap, pose with their trophy, the goose no doubt heading for the dinner pot.

Named
Displaying variations in civilian and military transitional uniforms, a large contingent of policeman pose for a group portrait that has been converted into a postcard. Presumably copies were made for each man, their individual names matched to the positions in the photograph. The front row of officers includes the designations for general inspectors and captains. While several wear decorations, including Iron Crosses and Wound Badges, they may be of First World War vintage as they are worn by the older men. Though the names are clearly listed, the location and date of the event are absent.

Police Barracks Professional Cooks
Wearing their service caps with distinctive police insignia, three mess hall staff members stir up the day's meal. In the last gasps of the war, they would be required to exchange their ladles for rifles, being sent into the maelstrom.

Shipping Out
A grim looking *polizei* and regular army (*Heer*) companion appear in a rail car window as they prepare to meet their new assignments. The larger ribbon bar worn by the army NCO indicates Iron Crosses won in both the First and Second World Wars, while the policeman's tunic shows an Iron Cross 2nd Class button decoration and the dual cuff stripes of a master sergeant.

Family Ties –
Separation of Duties

Family Outing
A high-ranking member of the police poses with his officially licensed automobile along with his well-dressed wife and son.

Family in the Garden
A mother sits among her family, including a First World War veteran and policeman father, the taller son an NCO in the *Grossdeutschland Schutzpolizei*, another in the Waffen-SS Panzer corps, and the youngest a member of the junior Hitler Youth (*Pimpf*). Only the mother and her daughter, the latter very likely in the BdM, are not in Third Reich uniform. Flower art and animal horns decorate what may be their vacation home.

Above left: **Big Brother**

Above right: **Generation Gap**
A policeman father poses with his Panzer trooper son, who looks rather askance at the camera.

Extended Family
A crouching policeman is the centre point for a group portrait. Three members of the German Army (*Heer*) are also present, the one holding a child apparently his brother, perhaps a twin.

Stylish Hats
Two women, perhaps mother and
daughter, appear in their furs and jaunty
headwear along with one civilian and two
men in uniform, the policeman wearing
what appears to be the popular mountain
troop-style soft cap.

**Dresden Dinnerware,
25 September 1942**
In the city Magdeburg, dinner guests
gather at a long table neatly set with
fine Dresden dinnerware. The variety of
guests include a woman with a dog in her
lap, civilians wearing Nazi Party pins or
First World War decorations, a decorated
Army NCO and a policeman with a lady
friend in the right foreground. A framed
portrait of the Fuhrer hangs on the wall.
   Magdeburg, the capital of Lower Saxony,
lies on the Elbe River in east central
Germany. A centre for the production of
synthetic oil during the war, it was heavily
bombed by the Allies, with much of the city
being destroyed by early 1945.

Gemutlichkeit
Sporting a traditional Prussian haircut,
an NCO medical staff policeman raises a
glass of *liebfraumilch* in a toast with his
dinner companion.

Eye Contact
A policeman and a young woman share a moment, hand in hand, at a table laden with pastries and coffee. What appear to be wine bottles frame a potted plant that holds a card, perhaps with their names. The man's suntanned wrist seems to indicate a wristwatch once worn during many hours in the sun. No rings are visible on either person's hands. A large shortwave radio is visible in the background.

Police Cavalry Troopers, 1942
What appear to be a mother and daughter sit atop horses, one a purebred Trakehner, apparently provided by two policemen, perhaps family members. The photo postcard was posted from Roggendorf, Austria, on 3 August 1942. At this time the German Sixth Army is advancing toward Stalingrad, entering it a few weeks later on 1 September, an event considered the beginning of the end for Nazi Germany.

Policeman with Two Sisters

Smiles for the Camera
A somewhat jovial trio of policemen pose for
the camera and have attracted a large crowd for
some reason, perhaps the cameraman's antics.
The plump *polizei* wears a campaign ribbon as
well as a silver Wound Badge, indicating two or
three wounds received – possibly a vestige of his
service in the First World War.

Two More Girls
Another photograph from the plump
policeman's album shows him with a fellow
officer and two new female additions. A clue
to the location can be seen in the photograph's
background, the large building apparently being
the Place Vendôme in Paris, where German
troops billeted en masse after its fall in the
summer of 1940.

Newlyweds
A *Gendarmerie* (rural policeman) poses with his new wife.
Protruding into the images is a baby carriage and a toddler,
who appears to be playing with a toy rifle.

Above left: **'Easter, March 1939' Reads the Notation on the Reverse.**
During this month, German forces occupy Moravia and Bohemia, now terming them 'protectorates'. The country of Czechoslovakia is wiped from the map.

Above right: **Policeman with Perambulator**
With his fashionably attired wife and equally fashionable baby carriage, a *polizei* wearing his *kepi*-style cap enjoys a peaceful country stroll.
    'I used to shoot at everything, certainly not just military targets. We liked to go for women pushing prams, often with children at their sides. It was a kind of sport really ...' So said *Oberleutnant* Hans Hartigs, a Luftwaffe fighter pilot, when confiding to a comrade about his strafing of civilians, his conversation secretly being recorded by British intelligence after he became a POW.

Left: **Anonymous Proud Policeman Poppa**
A member of the *Gendarmerie* wears the shoulder boards denoting a Precinct Staff Sergeant (*Revieroberwachtmeister*).

Casting a Shadow in the Darkness
A policeman sits stiffly in a chair while a large lamp harshly lights the scene. A lace-covered table beside him is carefully arranged with a vase of wildflowers, a cigarette lighter, cigarette dispenser and ashtray. His uniform displays only a sports badge.

Wound Badge and More Shadows
In a later photograph, the policeman now wears a Black Wound Badge, indicating an injury sustained on the battlefield. One hand holds the hand of his fidgeting baby held by his wife.

New Addition
Two police families have gathered for a dinner, perhaps to welcome the new baby. The older policeman wears a chest full of awards, including the Iron Cross and Wound Badge as well as a combat assault medal, which may be vestiges of his First World War service. Both men wear the formal decorative braided cord (*aiguillette*), which was phased out early in the war

Above left: **After Dinner Photo**
The same two families share an outdoor photo. The contrast in the couples' body language and expressions is obvious. The younger man holds a cigarette and the older policeman has the same expression as in the previous photo, while his son has donned his sailor's cap.

Above right: **Police Grandparent**
An elderly policeman and his wife appear to be out on a stroll with their grandson. The woman seems to be calling the child's attention to the camera.

Policeman's Postcard from Roggendorf, 1942

Police battalion members pose with a trio of women, two of whom are identified as 'Gudrun' and 'Lena' via typed notations on the reverse. The card was posted by one of the women to the family of one of the pictured men, a Martin Panzer from Hohenleuben, a city in the Thuringia district of Germany. The *polizei* appearing in the photo had served in Poland in 1942, where some 3 million Jewish citizens had been murdered, the killings beginning on the very first day of country's invasion on 1 September 1939.

The postcard, dated 18 August 1942, was posted from the village of Roggendorf, located 70 km west of Vienna, Austria. Roggendorf became the location for a subcamp of Mauthausen called Melk, code name 'Quartz', where approximately 8,000 male slave labourers worked in an underground ball-bearing factory. A day after the postcard was mailed, the Allies suffered a major disaster with the failed landing of British and Canadian troops at Dieppe on the French coast, with 4,000 of the 5,000 men being captured or killed.

Unflinching Gaze – Defeat Closing In, 1944

Dated 18 March 1944, during which German cities were being bombed into rubble, if not submission, the family portrait of a customs policeman bears the effects of time. At this point in the war the Allies were advancing up the Italian boot after the Anzio landings in January, while the Red Army continued to decimate German troops in the east, pushing them back toward Germany. The customs officer may soon be exchanging uniforms and sent to the front as the Third Reich began thrusting cooks, clerks, musicians *et al* into the carnage.

The day following the taking of the photo, Soviet troops reached the Carpathians, forcing German forces to withdraw. At this point Hitler also ordered the occupation of its Hungarian ally, resulting in the extermination of its 380,000 Jewish citizens.

Police Organisations –
Conscripts of the Police State

Innsbruck Policeman on Civilian DKW
With city police officers now assimilated into the Wehrmacht, the rider wears the distinctive green with brown cuff uniform worn by members of militarised police units. The location for the photo, according to the registration plate and notes on the reverse, indicate the Tyrolean Alpine city of Innsbruck, Austria, the country having been annexed into the Greater Reich by Nazi Germany in 1938.

A psychiatric hospital located in the town of Hall near Innsbruck housed hundreds of mentally and physically disabled patients. Considered 'unworthy lives' by the Third Reich, they were put to death under brutal conditions by the medical staff. During the September 2012 expansion of the hospital, its cemetery was forensically investigated, revealing the bodies over 200 murdered patients, often showing signs of beatings and broken bones prior to death.

Past in Pursuit of the Future
A civilian rural constable, wearing the traditional shako helmet and carrying both a briefcase and a rifle lags behind a *Wehrmacht Unteroffizier* (NCO), traveling aboard a larger machine. Both motorcycles are wearing black-out regulation headlamp covers, which indicates the war years. They are most likely in Germany itself, as indicated by the civilian policeman.

Vintage Toy Solider – BMW with *Polizei*
Detailed rendering of a 1930s BMW motorcycle as ridden by a member of the civilian police, who is depicted wearing the distinctive green uniform and a shako cap. Although horses and even bicycles carried battalions of German combatants, as did trucks and tracked vehicles, motorcycles often led the way: namely, purpose-made BMW and Zündapp military bikes as well as civilian models produced by NSU and DKW, plus a host of other brands.

Correct Insignia
The policeman wears the *polizei* insignia on the left arm of his uniform and carries a billy club. The 'P' of the front fender-mounted registration indicates *polizei*. German military motorcyclists played an important role as solo couriers and scouts, as teams of tank hunters or as divisions of fast-moving rifle troops. The German military eventually became the largest employer of motorcycles during the Second World War. Many private civilian motorcycles were eventually confiscated by the Nazi regime, with the owners frequently being inducted into the army simultaneously.

In Command – ZOLL Special *Aktion* Group
A general of the *Zentrale Unterstutzungsgruppe Zoll* (Central Customs Support Group special police unit) sits in his staff car as his adjutant, with briefcase in hand, stands by the open door. Members of the *Zollgrenzschutz* functioned as Customs Border Protection units.

Motorised Police – Rhineland Reoccupied
A group of Border Customs Protection Service soldiers equipped with a DKW motorcycle and a sidecar pose for their portrait somewhere in the Rhineland, as indicated by the license plate on their automobile. In violation of the First World War Versailles Treaty, Nazi Germany had reoccupied the Rhineland region on 7 March 1936.

Quick Response Firepower
The motorcycle sidecar supports a bipod-equipped Czech machine gun, while the man on the far left cradles a 9 mm submachine gun.

A Band for Every Occasion – Third Reich Fanfare
French horn, tubas, trombone, trumpets are all there as a police marching brass band refines its coordination. Martial music was seen as an integral component of morale and *esprit de corps*, while the incessant marching and physical activity was also designed to downplay intellectual introspection in favour of emotional response. Music was a constant background effect, being part of the intense sensory bombardment employed by the Nazi social planners to make the public malleable and keep their minds distracted. The mass production of inexpensive radios also, made available to almost every home, established Germany as the world's largest radio audience, a means by which Hitler brought his harangues to the largest possible audience.

The Church Mocked
On occasion, German troops were encouraged to mock religion, in this case while perhaps taking part in a police school graduation celebration. While Nazi social planners promoted their own pagan-inspired 'ideological' religion, many Germans, including policemen, were steadfast Catholics and Protestants.

Sermon of Sacrilege
Policemen enjoy the antics of two of their comrades, who have donned Russian Orthodox Church vestments and playact as priests. SS policemen were indoctrinated with the Nazi 'anti-Judeo-Christian' ideology and as a result would desecrate foreign houses of worship, both Jewish and Christian.

Policemen Ploughing
Three *polizei* have teamed up as tillers of a wheat field at an unspecified location.

Above left: **Olympian Heights – Strategic Gateway**
Twenty-three policeman have climbed high over the valley for a group portrait, an 'X' marking the soldier (far right) in whose album the photograph was kept. An inscription on the reverse reads, 'In remembrance of our first march near Nachod'. The location was the eastern Bohemian Czech town in the valley of the River Metuje, noted for its fourteenth-century castle as well as its town-owned brewery. The vantage point chosen by the policemen for their photo was the highest peak reachable from Nachod and known as Dobrosov. A number of Czech military bunkers and fortifications situated near Nachod were occupied by German forces after the occupation of the country. The town lay on the border of Poland and served as one the main launching points into that country.

Above right: **Field Police**
A member of the *Feldgendarmerie* assumes the 'present-arms' stance for the camera, the bolt action Mauser rifle being the standard German issue.

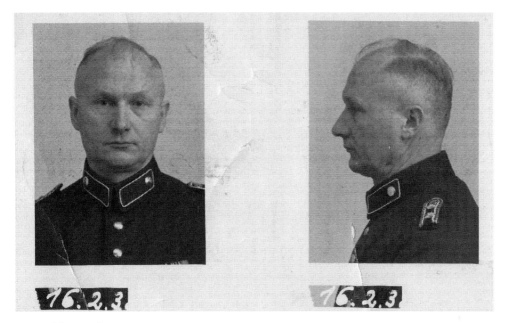

ID Card for a Policeman

Not all policemen were executioners; some functioned as true policemen, protecting German citizens from criminals and criminal acts. In fact, on occasion the police would even bring charges against the SS; for instance, the police investigated the corruption and brutality of Hilmar Wackerle, an early commandant of the Dachau concentration camp.

Located some 12 miles north-west of the Bavarian city of Munich, Dachau was initially created to incarcerate and 'educate' political opponents. The police charged Wackerle and his staff in the murder of camp inmates. This may seem odd, but it occurred early in the history of the Nazi takeover of the country and the victims were Aryan Germans as opposed to 'racial enemies' of the Third Reich. The prisoners' families caused a public uproar with ensuing negative publicity, much to the annoyance of Himmler and other party leaders. It should be remembered that a public outcry, including protests from both Catholic and Protestant German clergy, called for an end to the euthanasia program liquidating the mentally and physically handicapped. No such outcry resulted from the treatment of Germany's Jewish population.

Autographed Photograph from Goslar

Converted into a postcard, this image of policeman Erich Obermeyer was, according to the notations on the reverse, processed at the Herman Stumm 'Modern Portraiture Art' studio in Goslar, located in central Germany's Lower Saxony on the slopes of the Harz Mountains. Founded in the tenth century and based on the discovery of silver deposits, Goslar was also home to Heinz Guderian, the Third Reich's master tank tactician and post-war military official within West Germany and NATO. Goslar was also home to General Major Henning von Tresckow, the anti-Hitler conspirator who drafted the Valkyrie plan. When word reached him on the Eastern Front that the bomb plot against Hitler failed, Henning committed suicide by placing a grenade under his chin.

***Above left*: ID Photograph**

A *Schutzpolizei* smiles slightly for his official identification photo that would be pasted into his service record book. By July 1936 new police uniforms for the various police formations were standardised, being modelled after those of the German Army. The shoulder boards appeared in a variety of colour combinations (*Truppenfarbe*), although are difficult to distinguish due to the prevalent use of the black and white photos of the day.

***Above right*: ID Photograph: *Gendarmerie* Rural Policeman in Würzburg, November 1940**

This month saw the completion of a large-scale 'resettlement' program, whereby some 45,000 ethnic Germans, under the existing treaty with the Soviet Union, were relocated from Soviet-annexed Bessarabia and northern Bukovina to their new homes in German-occupied Poland as part of the Nazi plan to displace non-Aryans and repopulate the east with Nordic blood. A RAF bombing raid by 225 aircraft on 16 March 1945 devastated 90 per cent of Würzburg, with 5,000 civilians being killed. Post-war the many historical buildings were replicated, mostly by women workers over a period of twenty years.

ID Photograph – 'Popa'

When found, this small, tattered photograph had the word 'Popa' handwritten on its reverse. He wears the *Schutzpolizei* shoulder boards and a ribbon bar representing the awarding of the War Merit Badge with swords indicating bravery in combat but not sufficient to qualify for the Iron Cross 2nd Class.

***Above left*: Anomalies**
Much to the amusement of the taller policeman, and less to his shorter comrade, the two present themselves for a photo op. Despite the Nazi claims, not all German soldiers measured up to the epitome of the Aryan *Ubermensch*, the mythical Nordic 'Superman' destined to rule Pan-Europa and in the process enslave or eradicate the *Untermensch* – the inferior Slavs, the 'Asiatic' Bolsheviks and the 'pestilent Jews,' not to mention the 'physically unfit'.

***Above right*: Black Ice**
His comrades apparently enjoying his dilemma, a policeman slips on ice, the metal horseshoe heel and hobnails visible on his boot, while another captures the moment with his camera.

Keeping Pace in Hamburg
Younger members of the Hamburg police race toward the finishing line in a day of athletic rivalry. A carefully orchestrated mixture of competition and cohesion helped meld the police units into highly effective groups, many seeing action in front line combat.

'*Sportfest*' Competition as Training – Police Battalion 309

An officer apparently uses a megaphone to provide directions for a group of policemen, some of whom are relatively old and less physically fit. Many such non-front-line-quality individuals were assigned to the execution squads. Notations on the photograph's reverse identify the men as members of Company A, initially one of three formed in Cologne in 1940 as Police Battalion 309. On 27 June 1941, the 1st and 3rd Company of Order Police PB 309 joined the *Einsatzgruppen* in killing over 3,000 Jews in Bialystok, including some 800 being locked in the city's synagogue, which was then set ablaze. Several PB 309 members received awards for their actions and several resumed their police work in post-war Germany.

Bialystok was Polish until the 1939 German-Russian joint invasion of Poland, when it was integrated into Soviet Belarus (Byelorussian SSR). This lasted until 1941, when Germany invaded the USSR, with the city then again being part of German-occupied Poland. 56,000 Jewish residents were then forced into the Bialystok Ghetto and, when scheduled for liquidation, with its members being transported to the Treblinka Death Camp, several hundred Jews and members of the Polish anti-fascist military rose up in revolt. Though poorly armed against the German forces, they held out for a week. It was another year before Red Army forces liberated the city.

Manpower *v.* Horsepower

A mounted policeman apparently competes in a relay race against a comrade racing on foot during a public demonstration in the city of Saarbrücken.

Exercises in Solidarity – Saarbrücken

Policemen wearing their traditional helmets along with their Third Reich uniforms perform for an audience in the city of Saarbrücken. One of their comrades is captured mid-tumble as he vaults over his comrades, who demonstrate their disciplined control. Spotters await the gymnast's landing.

Saarbrücken, the capital of the Saarland in south-eastern Germany, and adjacent to the French border, was notable as an industrial and transportation centre due to its coal reserves, and as a result was an important resource for German war production.

Variation on a Theme

A policeman somersaults over the backs of three horses with the aid of a gymnast's ramp.

Instruction in Apprehension Techniques

Instructions on the proper means of subduing and searching a prisoner are demonstrated during an outdoor session, the distinctive police emblem now visible on the left tunic sleeve and cap.

Chewing Out
During an inspection of their field kits, which are seen strewn out behind the recruits, an NCO harangues one unhappy-looking fellow about some infraction as his comrades look on with their bootless feet. As his right hand seems to be in motion, the instructor may about to fling something at the offending recruit.

The Austrian Connection – 'Yes for the Fuehrer' – Vienna Post Office
In 1938 police battalions participated in the annexation of Austria (*Anschluss*) and the occupation of the Sudetenland in 1939. Later that year, during the invasion of Poland, police units took on duties of deportations and mass executions in addition to their work of policing and internal security. During the first year of the war, over 100 police battalions were in operation as the forefront 'political soldiers' enforcing the racial war in the east. Hitler himself was Austrian by birth and the country's endemic anti-Semitism was often more virulent than in Germany.

'Greetings from Austria', 1938
Policemen have decorated their transport with graffiti, including above the windshield, which reads 'Return to Mother'. The photo coincides with the March 1938 *Anschluss*, when the Third Reich 'absorbed' Austria into the Greater Reich.

Above left: On Duty in Vienna, 18 March 1938
Six days after the *Anschluss* a young policeman poses for a photo amidst a busy pedestrian street scene. Meanwhile, another policeman appears to be checking papers in the far left background. Swastika banners decorate the buildings behind. Oddly, two nuns and a man in orthodox Jewish clothing also appear in the photograph.

Above right: Vienna Souvenir, 1938
Two field policemen pose before the Hofburg, the palatial complex at the heart of Vienna that for over 600 years served as the residence of the Austrian imperial rulers, including the Habsburgs, who reigned from the thirteenth century until the end of the monarchy in 1918. The equestrian statue in the background is of Prince Eugene of Savoy, a Frenchmen who aligned himself with the Austrian Empire, winning them extensive military victories from 1683 through the 1720s.

Transition in Vienna
Two policemen pose before a car showing a Luftwaffe (WL) license plate as a contingent of *Luftschutz* air defence troops stand in the background, having disembarked from their trucks for the photo op. Here, differences in headgear illustrate the transformation of civilian police into militarised police.

***Above left*: Fun with Fisticuffs**
Policemen have joined the spectators of a boxing match. A 'time keeper' notes the rounds by clanging on a metal food pot.

***Above right*: Austrian Vantage Point in Poland**
Somewhere in Poland, *Gebirgsjäger* (mountain troops) manage to ascend to some height. Some wear combat assault badges, while the individual in the foreground shows a button ribbon indicating the Iron Cross 2nd Class.

Berlin Police Station Nerve Centre
A number of uniformed and plainclothes police officers and officials have gathered for a photo in the Lichtenberg district. The walls carry maps and kitsch artwork. What appears to be a large wall safe is visible in the far right background. The various organisations charged with specific duties included the *Orpo*, or regular police, the *Sipo*, or security police, and the *Kripo*, or criminal police, the abbreviations for *Ordnungspolizei*, *Sicherheitspolizei* and *Kriminalpolizei* respectively.

Pre-War Relaxation, April 1939
The war still five months away, four
policemen enjoy their newspapers
while sitting on matching chairs. Three
wear DRL (*Deutscher Reichsbund
Leibes* – German National Physical
Education Union) sports badges. In this
month, German Jews were required
to turn over all their valuables, the
battleship *Tirpitz* was launched, the
'Death's Head' *SS-Totenkopfverbande*
formation was formalised and Franco's
fascist forces, supported by Nazi
Germany's military, announced final
victory over Republican forces in the
Spanish Civil War, in effect the prelude
to the Second World War.

Off-Duty
A mix of policemen includes two
members of the *Schutzpolizei des
Gemeinden* (municipal police) in
the lighter colour uniforms (centre),
their collar tabs indicating the rank
of *Hauptwachtmeister* (Sgt Major).
The *Gendarmerie* corporal in the left
foreground shows his cards to the
camera and appears to be working on
a straight – perhaps the winning hand
if the game is poker. The other players
appear to be members of the field
police. No money is visible on the table
since gambling is illegal in the Third
Reich, especially among the police.

**Portrait with a Fern Tree in the
Town of Friesack**
A policeman in his formal uniform,
including a ceremonial sword,
holds a dog leash while posing
with his *Schutzhund*, who wears
an ornate collar. The photograph
was processed in the small town of
Friesack in north-eastern Germany.
With a population of some 3,600 in
1939, it would attain notoriety for
the establishment of a special POW
camp where Irishmen serving in the
British military were recruited by
German intelligence and military,
appealing to Irish nationalists resisting
British occupation.

Above left: **Policeman and Police Dog**
Dogs were an integral tool of police units as well as concentration camp personnel, where they were employed to both track down victims and to maintain an atmosphere of terror.

Above right: **In the East**
Haggard-looking police are joined by a dog tethered to their wooden-wheeled horse cart, which is loaded with supplies.

Search and Destroy – A Week after the Wansee Conference
A *Gendarmerie* duo and their dog make their way through deep snow. An official German press release photograph dated 27 January 1942 reads: 'For field patrols through the thick forest terrain, the field gendarmes have trained with search dogs.' One week earlier, on the 20th, the infamous meeting held in the Berlin suburb of Wansee formulated the 'Final Solution', the Nazi hierarchy's determination to annihilate the 11 million Jews of Europe. Within a few weeks the first death camps were under construction in Poland.

Above left: **Hunter of Men**

A member of the Field Police (*Feldgendarmerie*) wears non-standard headgear to withstand the Russian winter cold, yet his overcoat will prove less than adequate. Hitler had predicted that the USSR would 'fall like a rotten house of cards' within a few months. So assured were the German generals that they failed to equip their troops with adequate clothing and equipment. As a result, tens of thousands, dressed in thin summer uniforms, would pay the price exacted by Russia's historical ally, 'General Winter', when temperatures fell to -30° F, freezing both men and machines.

Above right: **Field Police Armed**

A *Feldgendarmerie* troop, outfitted in their white denim fatigues, prepares for manoeuvres. One carries a Czech-made ZB vs. 26 machine gun firing 7.9 mm cartridges at 500 RPM from its twenty-round box magazine. Such units engaged in anti-partisan, anti-Jewish actions and also front line battles as the war ground up regular combat troops.

Armed Postmen

Notations on the reverse of the photograph read '*Postschutz – Kameradschaften der Deutsche. Reichpost (Pakpostamt Dresden 7, Kunad Strasse) als Feldpost an der Ostfront*', indicating their comradeship as members of the *Postschutz* and their duties at the Dresden post office, as well as safeguarding mail from the Eastern Front. The security of postal offices and the flow of millions of letters and parcels to and from the Front was the responsibility of the 4,500 members of the postal police, or *Postschutz*.

***Above left*: Maintaining Communications at Home and in the Field**
The *Postschutz* were also tasked with the security of lines of communication at home and the Front. Seen here, one man has climbed the telegraph or telephone pole, while another standing beneath unreels a small roll of wire worn around his neck. Another stands guard, rifle at the ready.

***Above right*: Polizei Nachtrichten**
A communications unit poses with their state-of-the-art mobile electronics centre on their way to an *aktion*, as noted on the reverse of the photo taken in 1941. The vehicle is an Einheits-Diesel, which was used as a base for a variety of practises, including as darkrooms and for carrying devices used for detecting enemy broadcasting.

Police Communications Squad on Practice March
Rather than rifles, a squad of privates wearing their denim fatigues carries field communication gear along a dirt road. What at first glance appear to be rifles are actually mounting poles.

Above left: **Police Field Communications in Action**
A trio of policemen confer as their comrade attempts to establish contact via a field telephone after laying
down the cable from the spool seen in the foreground. Cable layers were prime targets for snipers because
of their importance in maintaining battlefield communication. The spurs on their boots identify the group as
members of the cavalry mounted police.

Above right: **Danzig and Entry into War**
A policeman (right) poses with an Army NCO (far left) and corporal somewhere in Danzig, the city having
been annexed by Germany on 2 September 1939, the day after the invasion of Poland. As a result of the First
World War Treaty of Versailles, the ethnically German port had previously functioned as an independent
city state under the supervision of the League of Nations. Although surrounded by Polish territory, by 1933,
and Hitler's rise to power, a large percentage of its residents wished for the city to return to the Reich, and
as a result the Nazi Party secured 38 per cent of parliament. Hitler's strategy was to use Danzig as an excuse
to attack Poland. Feverishly virulent anti-Polish propaganda helped pave the way, followed by 1,000 SS
troops who 'infiltrated' under the guise of a sporting event. While Hitler's henchmen pretended to continue
negotiations with Poland, Germany forces prepared to strike.

Toasting Victory, 1940
With lightning victories in both
Poland and France, Germany
seems unstoppable. A group of
policemen toast each other and
their accomplishments with a
bottle of French Cointreau.

Above left: **France: SS Police, 1940**
Standing in a French rose garden, three members of the regular Field Police confer with two SS-*Schutzpolizei*, as indicated by the SS lightning bolt insignia worn by the man on the right who seems to be exchanging eye contact with his non-SS opposites, though they appear to take his intense expression lightly. In addition to serving in the field as executioners, members of the SS police also operated in the death camps.

Above left: *Feldgendarmerie* **at the Eiffel Tower, 16 August 1942**
This souvenir photo postcard was taken by untold numbers of German soldiers. Visible through the base of the Eiffel Tower are the colonnades of the 1936 Paris World Exhibition. The field policeman's uniform shows a DRL sports badge, Iron Cross 2nd ribbon and an Infantry Assault Badge in silver, indicating three or more infantry assaults, counter-attacks or reconnaissance operations. The day after the photograph was taken, eighteen American B-17E's bombed Rouen-Sotteville, France, marking the beginning of USAAF daylight raids on German-occupied Europe.

Bomb Damage in France
A pair of Field Police inspects damage to buildings as a French civilian looks on. It is uncertain if the damage was incurred during the German summer 1940 invasion or Allied bombing later in the war. In the final count American air attacks killed more French civilians than the Germans.

Police Collaboration
In an official German press photo, an SS NCO goes over plans with a Parisian gendarme. A long festering subject has been the collaboration of the city's police with the infamous round-up of Jewish civilians. Moreover, while the Germans had ordered the collection of adult men and women, the French constabulary on their own initiative included children. Eventually, some 79,000 Jews were sent to the death camps. In addition, the French also established their own version of the German Gestapo, naming it the *Melice*. Aiding the Germans in their anti-Resistance and anti-Jewish actions, its agents murdered thousands and regularly tortured its prisoners to a level that even the Gestapo found offensive. Some 25,000 Frenchmen joined their ranks, motivated by far-right political leanings or to escape petty crime jail sentences, or else by the lure of money, extra food rations or anger with the destruction and French casualties caused by Allied bombings.

Above left: **Hearts and Minds**
As his comrade records the moment with his camera, a *polizei* appears to be examining a French child's collection of eggs. After completing their six-week conquest of France in April 1940, and as a result of the armistice, the Germans divided France between the German-occupied north and left the south in the hands of a collaborationist government headquartered in Vichy under Marshall Henri Petain. Thereafter, France was officially neutral but bound by its agreements with Germany.

Above right: **Give and Take**
Another *polizei* is either removing or adding an egg to the young child's collection.

Narvik, Norway, in 1940

Policemen have gathered at the Narvik railway station, one wearing the anti-partisan warfare badge and others the polished metal gorget chestplate identifying their police status.

Germany competed with Britain for control of the Scandinavian countries' strategic iron ore supplies. During the winter of 1939/40, one of the coldest in history, more than 9 million tons of iron ore were also shipped from neighbouring Sweden. Throughout the war the Swedish government maintained a policy of neutrality – a successful stance for more than a century. It was one of only five European countries able to remain neutral during the Second World War, in part due to its geographic position.

The German and British navies first clashed in Narvik in April 1940, the Royal Navy winning the engagement, putting out of action nine destroyers, or 50 per cent of the *Kriegsmarine* destroyer fleet. Britain and its allies won the day, but only temporarily. German forces would ultimately gain control of Narvik and the rest of Norway (and Denmark), but its naval losses helped to blunt Hitler's plans to invade England.

Oslo, Norway, 1942

German policemen immediately followed German troop occupations. Here a group, including a particularly large individual, poses in Oslo. A notation states the date as 30 June 1942, just twenty days after they overwhelmed Allied resistance and took control of the neutral country.

During the assault on Norway, German forces sustained 1,300 KIA, while Norwegian losses were 850 killed, British losses were 4,000 and some 530 combined French and Polish forces were killed. German police battalions later took part in crushing Norwegian resistance, with thousands jailed or sent to concentration camps. Of its 1,800 Jewish residents, about half were able to flee to Sweden. Though originally posted in Norway, members of the 9th Police Battalion were temporarily reassigned to three of the *Einsatzgruppen*, who began shooting Jewish civilians in Russia as of June 1941 on the heels of the German invasion.

Oslo, Norway, Occupation in 1940
A German soldier's camera captures the action as troops and a policeman in black congregate in front of the Norwegian capital's parliament house. Norwegian forces fought for sixty-two days against the German onslaught – the longest period of resistance after the Soviet Union. However, this resulted in the sinking or capture of 107 Norwegian ships. Members of the Norwegian STAPO (state police) collaborated with the German SD (*Sicherheitspolizei*), with some 50,000 Norwegians being arrested during the occupation, 9,000 of which were sent to prison camps. A major anti-Nazi operation undertaken by Norwegian commandos disrupted the German nuclear bomb program by destroying its heavy water production facility.

Schutzpolizei Officer Poses with an American Car, January 1941
Recruited as a staff car, the sporty Buick convertible's 'streamlined' fender-embedded headlights have been 'blacked out' as required by wartime regulations. The policeman's tunic displays the Iron Cross 2nd ribbon, an Assault Badge and a Wound Badge apparently in silver – awards perhaps gained from his actions in the Polish and/or French campaigns.

Police Snowman
The winter months of January and February 1941 saw Germany establishing the *Afrika Korps* under the command of General Erwin Rommel, initially to come to the aid of their Italian fascist allies floundering in North Africa when facing British forces.

***Above left*: Formal Portrait – 'In Remembrance of Passau', 2 March 1941**
On this very day, German troops march into Bulgaria to take control of the Balkans, with the invasion of the Soviet Union planned to commence in June. In addition to his Iron Cross 1st Class, the policeman's ribbon bar indicates service in several campaigns. His handwritten inscription on the reverse of the photo postcard reads: 'In remembrance – Passau on 2 March1941 – Alois Freiberger.'

Passau, a town in Lower Bavaria, was briefly home to Adolf Hitler and his family (1892–94) as well as for SS *Reichsführer* Heinrich Himmler. The area later supported three sub-camps of the Mauthausen–Gusen concentration camp. The SS nicknamed the camp 'Bonegrinder' as it was designed specifically to exterminate its inmates through backbreaking work. Estimates of death range from some 130,000 to 320,000 for the complex of camps.

***Above right*: Stopover in Mauthausen, Austria: The War at Intersections, 26 May 1941**
In a festive mood, policemen joined by their female companions have their photo taken by a cattle car, such as those used to transport victims to the death camps.

May 1941 saw Reinhard Heydrich, head of the Reich Security Service and architect of Operation Reinhard, aka the Final Solution, instructing his *Einsatzkommando* leaders in preparation for the invasion of the Soviet Union scheduled for the following month. He orders the extermination of all Jews, communist officials, the intelligentsia, gypsies and 'Asiatics'. On the day following this photograph, the famous German battle cruiser *Bismarck* was sunk by the Royal Navy, while on the same day Greece surrendered to German forces.

Mauthausen and its many subcamps were among the most successful financial operations conducted by Himmler's SS, earning millions for the Third Reich. The slave labourers were forced to carry heavy quarry stones weighing as much as 120 lbs on their backs while climbing the near-vertical 186 steps to the top of *Der Himmelsweg* (Path to Heaven), until they eventually died from the exertion – accelerated by starvation and the guards' brutality. Several US airmen POWs suffered the same fate.

Above left: Bi-Lingual Balkans – *Polizei/Policia*
Police guard the entrance to their impromptu station
established in Albania. After Mussolini's blunder into
the Balkans necessitated Germany's intervention, its
troops occupied Albanian airports and ports, and
eventually the entire country in September 1943. As
a result regular military and police units engaged the
partisan and communist resistance groups in brutal
fighting. Although the Germans tried to establish
an autonomous state supporting Germany, the
partisans prevailed and wrested complete control of
the country by the end of November 1944. When
followed by Soviet advances into the area, German
forces withdrew, with the country then falling under
communist control.

Above right: Cuff-Title
Three *polizei*, two in denim fatigues, pose for the
camera. The uniformed soldier's sleeve displays
a so-called 'cuff-title', in this case stitched with
Deutsche Wehrmacht, identifying German police
personnel operating alongside German armed
forces outside the borders of the Reich.

Right: Luftwaffe Policeman
The airman *Gefreiter* (corporal) wears the police
emblem below his rank chevron on his left
forearm. All branches of the Wehrmacht contained
police units to enforce military and state rules and
regulations.

Snowbound
Three *polizei* brave the cold for a better view and a photo op. The soldier on the right carries the standard messenger's leather pouch alongside his bayonet.

Tour of Inspection
A contingent of policemen visit a shipyard. The three men in the foreground display the Nazi 'political' versions of the standard German sports badges on their tunics.

'Desk Killer'
All aspects of the Germany military kept meticulous records, including the mass murders committed by the various police organisations. Some of these records later served in indicting the perpetrators in post-war investigations.

Perſonalbogen

des **R i c h t e r , Ludwig**
Name _Vornamen (Rufnamen unterſtreichen)_

Polizei= **Meiſter der Gendarmerie**
Amtsbezeichnung

geboren am **26.5.1898** in **Bodensee**
Tag, Monat, Jahr _Ort_

Duderſtadt Relig. Bekenntnis: **kath.**
Kreis

Familienſtand: ~~ledig~~ — verheiratet ſeit **30.8.1925** mit
Tag, Monat, Jahr

Auguſte Werner verwitwet — geſchieden ſeit
Vor- und Elternname der Ehefrau

; wiederverheiratet am mit
Tag, Monat, Jahr

Vor- und Elternname der Ehefrau

Kinder:

Name	geboren	Name	geboren
Helmuth	27.9.24		
Waltraud	25.9.26		
Margit	3.1.28		
Ludwig	2o.9.33		
Jürgen	8.1o.43		

Geſtalt: **mittel**
Körpergröße: **1,73**
Sportliche Veranlagung: **Leichtathlet**
Körperliche Veranlagung: **geſund kräftig**

Deutſchblütige Abſtammung des Beamten: ja — ~~nein~~ ſ. Unterordner B Bl.
der Ehefrau: ja — ~~nein~~ ſ. Unterordner B Bl.

Mitglied der NSDAP. und ihrer Gliederungen: | **Ehrenzeichen der NSDAP.:** ----

NSDAP. ſeit **1.5.1933** Mitgl.-Nr. **2 857 8o5**
HJ. ſeit „
SA. ſeit „
ℋ ſeit „
NSKK. ſeit „
NSV. ſeit **1.5.1935** „ **3 986 142**
ſeit „
ſeit „

Führerſtellung innerhalb der Bewegung: ----

Zugehörigkeit zu

früheren politiſchen Parteien uſw.			früheren Beamtenvereinen uſw.		
Bezeichnung	vom	bis	Bezeichnung	vom	bis
----			Verband Preuß.Landj.	1.1o.	1933
			Beamten	193o	

Logen uſw. (auch Angabe über den erreichten Grad)			jetzigen Beamtenorganiſationen		
Bezeichnung	vom	bis	Bezeichnung	vom	bis
----			Kam.-Bund Dt.Pol.Beamt.	1933	

DIN A 3
297 × 420 mm
Vordruck
R. Pol. Nr. 10

Personalbogen – Personal File – *Schutzpolizei*
This rare document from the files of the *Schutzpolizei* chronicles the service record of Ludwig Richter. The document noted him as being born on 5 May 1898 in Duderstadt in central Germany. Richter, whose education consisted of elementary schooling, was described as middle sized, athletic (holder of a SA sports badge) and 'vigorously healthy'. He listed himself as a member of the Catholic faith, married and the father of five children, four boys and one girl: Helmuth, Waltraud, Margit, Ludwig and Jurgen. His wife's name was not listed.

File Photos – Profile of a Policeman

During the First World War, Richter was wounded on the front line while serving as a corporal in the foot artillery. Joining the civilian police in 1921, attaining the rank of sergeant, he joined the Nazi Party (#2857805) on 5 January 1933, four days after Hitler assumed power. On 15 February 1938, he joined the military police in the town of Hanau, located 25 km east of Frankfurt-am-Main, attaining the rank of *Gendarmerie-Meister* on 12 January 1941.

When the Second World War began, his oldest son, Helmuth, had recently turned fifteen and may have seen military service, as would have his brother, Waltraud, aged thirteen in September 1939. Three of the children were born in the month of September, indicating a pattern of home leave. The last born and therefore youngest, Jurgen, was born on 8 November 1943, two days after Soviet forces recaptured the city of Kiev in the Ukraine, with Germany now being on the defensive, from which it would never recover. During his military police service Richter was awarded the Iron Cross 2nd and 1st Class, a Combat Assault Badge and a Wound Badge in black. There are no further entry dates after August 1943, which could indicate his death.

Night Watch

Lit by lamplight and joined by a man in civilian clothes, a fellow policeman is captured by a comrade's camera. The railway security policeman (*Bahnschutzpolizei*) appears busy on the phone while jotting in a logbook, the desk occupied by an inkwell, a telephone with extension buttons, a blotter roller to dry ink, and a cigarette ash tray. The uniformed man in the window, a *Gendarmerie* NCO, wears his overseas cap and a service ribbon. A colour photo would reveal his collar tabs have a red-orange base colour.

Above left: **Always on Schedule – Railway Police**
Reichsbahn policemen guarded the trains against sabotage and helped ensure that civilian and troop trains ran on precise schedules. Additionally, they directly contributed to the efficient orchestration of the thousands of trains funnelling Jews to the death camps, without which the Holocaust could not have proceeded.

Above right: *Deutsche Wehrmacht* **Armband, 1 July 1941**
Part-time police officers serving as guardians of the rail system via the *Bahnschutzpolizei* were also tasked with anti-sabotage duties as well as guarding POW and concentration camp transport trains. Some eight days prior to the date of this photo, the fateful Operation Barbarossa had been launched against the Soviet Union and by July the SS-*Einsatzgruppen* special police units, under orders from Göring, had already begun the systematic extermination of the Soviet Jewish population.

Organisation Todt Security
A policemen serving within the OT, or Organisation Todt, stands before what may be a barracks, although a barbed wire fence is visible and may indicate that the building houses 'foreign labourers' – millions brought from occupied territories to Germany either through volunteering and the promise of food or by force so they could toil in factories and mines.

The OT was a special division set up in 1933 to construct military installations (including the Western Wall) and the autobahn superhighways designed for the movement of heavy mobile armour. After its founding director, Dr Fritz Todt, died in a somewhat mysterious airplane accident in February 1942, Albert Speer took over control as Reich Minister of Armaments and implemented nearly miraculous improvements to war production, effectively extending Germany's ability to continue fighting despite depletion of resources and non-stop Allied bombing.

Motorised Police
A group of policemen gather outside their barracks for a group portrait alongside one of their motor pool vehicles. Somehow a civilian, perhaps a mechanic, has introduced himself into the photo session.

Pilsen Police, 1940
Band members play during an athletic demonstration performed at a gathering of police in Pilsen. After the Sudetenland was 'peacefully' occupied by German forces in March 1939, Pilsen became a temporary refuge for many Jews fleeing from the surrounding communities. However, the desecration of the city's Jewish cemetery and the murder of community's rabbi in 1940 were followed by deportations of the city's 3,200 Jews to the death camps.

Master of his World in Pilsen, 1940
A *polizei* sits atop a miniature waterfall in Lochoton Park, the tourist attraction found in the German-occupied Czech Bohemian city of Pilsen. Dated February 1940, handwritten notations on the reverse read 'In remembrance of my comrades Rohrmus and Lohmedelbach.' In this month German U-boat wolf packs were decimating Allied shipping in the North Atlantic and in Germany, while the first German Jews were being deported, with 160,000 being eventually sent to the camps.

***Above left*: Idyllic Moment**
A policeman has his photo snapped at a dam's artificial waterfall, over which runs a catwalk bridge. Nazi political rhetoric included a semi-pagan return to nature and established various organisations that encouraged nature walks and protecting the environment. Official recognition of this policy appeared in 1935 with the Reich Nature Protection Law (*Reichsnaturschutzgesetz* or RNG). Göring also promoted the national protection of German forests and habitats, perhaps prompted by his frequent hunting parties. In general, the protection of German's natural landscape was integrated into the overall Nazi mindset of *Volksgemeinschaft* (Blood and Soil). In the final analysis the environment was plundered for its natural resources, both locally and in occupied lands, all toward fuelling the German war machine.

***Above right*: Policemen on Leave Enjoy a Boat Ride**

Bicycle Comic
His uniform sleeve's cuff indicating a special unit, a *polizei* entertains his friends, and the cameraman, with his antics. One automobile carries a 'Pol' license plate, identifying it as a police vehicle.

***Above left*: Bicycle Policeman**

During the First World War, the bicycle soldier had literally been the fastest mobile force on the battlefield. The German blitzkrieg tactics of the Second World War would shunt the cycle troops aside from that leading role, but they would assume other tasks in the wake of the Panzers rolling over Polish defences at the outbreak of war. In particular they took part in mopping up operations and via speedy pursuit prevented the Polish infantry, now totally on foot, from regrouping into cohesive fighting units. When Hitler viewed his victorious troops in Warsaw on 5 October 1939, among the elite units paraded before him were the cycle troops of the Volks Grenadier Division.

***Above right*: Making his Rounds**

A bicycle-riding policeman stops for a chat with a friend carrying a child's doll. The fact that the policeman has removed his right glove, indicative of a handshake, is evidence that a friendly conversation is in progress. Perhaps it is merely a coincidence, but the doll seems to be giving the mandatory Hitler salute.

Mapping Out Hamburg

His face lit by bright sunlight from a window, a policeman has himself photographed in front of a large wall map of Hamburg, the only legible notations being *Gruppe Ost*, or Group East. He may be in charge of police operations in the city. The photograph was processed at the Wiesenhavern specialty photography shop then located in Hamburg and still in operation today.

Above left: *Gendarmerie* with Unknown Duties

Above right: No Age Limit
Older, physically less able policemen were often sent to the execution squads.

Right: Old School SS
Another veteran SS policeman with smoke-stained teeth smiles for the camera. His tunic is pinned with SS lightning runes, an SA sports badge and a close combat medal. Many policeman were over forty, while others were too young for regular combat service and so served as concentration camp guards or as members of execution squads. Some were also culled from the ranks of the wounded and disabled.

Above left: **The Green and the Grey – 'The Police on the Front Line'**
A commercial postcard issued to commemorate the 1942 Day of the Police dramatises the coordination of the *Ordnungspolizei* (regular police) and the *Sicherheitspolizei* (security police). The *Orpo* man carries a standard infantry rifle while the SS man carries a MP32 Bergman submachine gun, as issued to special units. This is considered the first submachine gun used in combat.

Above right: **Directions to SS Police**
A 'sign tree' has sprouted in a Polish city with directions to a variety of offices, staging areas and housing, as well as the local military hospital and the commander's headquarters for the SS *Polizei-Führer* of the *Ordnungspolizei*. The police leaders commanded the death squads in Poland and the Soviet Union and oversaw the ghettos and deportations to the death camps.

High-Ranking SS *Polizei* Takes Aim
Firing the iconic Luger P08 pistol at a target range, the officer's brown cuffs also display the SS lightning bolt runes, a long service badge and a Wound Badge in black, indicating a single wound. His collar tabs (gold insignia/green background) establish his rank as a police general.

SS *Polizei*
SS policemen smile at the cameraman. The decorated officer on the right wears the SS runes on his uniform next to his Wound Badge and Iron Cross 1st Class. While some police units fought in combat, thus earning their decorations, special medals were also created for actions against partisans and other 'criminal elements' targeted by Nazi political and racial policies.

Above left: **SS *Feldgendarmerie***
A member of the Field Police has signed his studio portrait. He wears the distinctive polished metal gorget chest emblem denoting his powers to arrest anyone regardless of rank. In April 1943, *Reichsführer*-SS Himmler mandated the title of 'SS Police Regiments' to all police formations, in keeping with the merging of the civilian police and the SS as one unified force and thus under his ultimate control.

Above right: **Rudolf Pannier – 4th SS *Polizei Panzergrenadier***
Pannier held the rank of *Oberst* (colonel) of the Waffen-SS Police (4th SS *Polizei Panzergrenadier*) Division of Army Group North and 14th Waffen Grenadier Division of the SS Galicia (1st Ukrainian). During the invasion of the Soviet Union, as a *Hauptman* (captain) he was awarded the Iron Cross 2nd and 1st Class, then the Knight's Cross for bravery in combat when in command of the 2nd SS *Polizei Schutzen* Regiment. In 1943 he commanded a Waffen SS anti-partisan unit in the Minsk area, followed by command of a Waffen Grenadier Regiment near war's end. Wounded in April 1945, as a result he ended up addicted to morphine. He lived until eighty-one, dying in Hamburg in 1978.

***Above left*: Commemorative Third Reich Stamp for Reinhard Heydrich, Protector of Bohemia and Moravia**
Appointed by *Reichsführer*-SS Heinrich Himmler on 7 September 1939, as an SS *Obergruppenführer*
Heydrich served as Chief of the Security Police and the Security Service, or SD, until his assassination
at age thirty-eight by British-trained Czech commandos in June 1942. Although he was a favourite of
Hitler, Heydrich was so detested that his death was even celebrated by several high-ranking Nazis. Ernst
Kaltenbrunner took over Heydrich's position on 30 January 1943, retaining the post until the end of the
war, after which the SD was declared a criminal organisation and its members were tried as war criminals.
During the Nuremberg Trials, Kaltenbrunner stated, 'I do not feel guilty of any war crimes.' As he was
hanged, he called out, 'Good luck, Germany.'

***Above right*: Intimate Moment**
An SS/SD man with the cuff title of the *Grenz-Polizei* (Frontier Police) sits with a member of the
Customs Police.

***Sicherheitsdienst* Policeman at Work**
In this photo an SD man, submachine gun hung over his shoulder, checks a Russian peasant's documents.
A corporal of the police standing nearby wears the close combat badge on his tunic pocket and around his
neck is the insignia of the military police. Nicknamed 'The Chain Dogs', they were often held in contempt
and feared by the regular soldiers over whom they held total power of arrest.

Dinner Party
An *Hauptscharführer* (senior NCO) of the SD appears sandwiched between two sisters and their mother, he himself perhaps a brother or married to one of the sisters. The table is set with fine Dresden china, as well as cookies, pastries, a large coffee pot and a decanter of liqueur. A calendar on the wall indicates the 31st of the month, though which month is it and which year is unknown.

Killer Elite – SD/SS Target Practice
In uniform and civilian clothing, officials of the SD and the SS, some armed with submachine guns, stand before a munitions bunker. They may be test firing the weapons at unknown targets, with one SD member apparently recording notes.

Aktions in the Field – Eastern Europe and Russia

'*Zmarla*' – The Double Murder of Poland – 1939

'Welcome to Poland!'
German soldiers have expressed their opinion of Poland. Years of Nazi-produced virulent propaganda had demonised and degraded the Poles into *untermenschen* status, preparing the way for the planned destruction of Polish culture.

Germany launched its attack on Poland from the west on 1 September 1939 followed, on 17 September, by communist Russia attacking the country from the east as a result of the Molotov-Ribbentrop Pact of 23 August 1939 when the avowed enemies agreed to carve up the country. The Soviets then began a wave of terror against Polish politicians, priests, military leaders and police, with thousands being killed and hundreds of thousands more being deported to Siberia. As a result of the June 1941 invasion of the USSR, the communist forces fled Poland, with the entirety of Poland falling under the swastika. Even its name was excised, with it now being known as the *Generalgouvernement*.

Two Generations, October 1939
Veteran and young policeman have gathered for a group portrait, which will be transformed into a mailable postcard. The event is noted as taking place on 5 October 1939, one month after the invasion of Poland. At the beginning of October, German forces were finalising their blitzkrieg victory over Poland, in the process losing 10,572 KIA as compared to Polish losses of some 50,000 killed, with another 750,000 taken as POWs. The occupation of Poland was part of the strategic plan to dominate by force all non-German speaking lands – a stepping stone to world military and industrial domination. The motivational concept was *Lebensraum*, or the acquisition of increased living space for the citizens of the Third Reich, including the vast agricultural lands and natural resources of the Soviet Union. This involved the 'relocation' of the indigenous people either through mass extermination via programmed starvation or their enslavement to the needs of Nazi Germany.

City Gates, Kraków, Poland
Two policemen pose for their portrait while a priest holding packages gets caught in the photo op. As part of the Nazi plan to destroy Polish culture, the SS would soon set about imprisoning or murdering large numbers of the country's religious leaders. Kraków, Poland's second largest and oldest city (seventh century), became the capital of the German-controlled General Government. Its Jewish citizens were forced into a ghetto, before then being transported to the death camps or to Płaszów, the 200-acre concentration and labour camp the Germans had constructed on the grounds of two former Jewish cemeteries. While its guards were mostly Ukrainian, one of the camp's commandants, Austrian Amon Göth, violated even SS rules of conduct and was removed from his post and assessed as mentally ill. After the Allies' post-war trail he was executed for his many crimes, including his personal murder of men, women and children on a daily basis. The embodiment of Nazi cruelty and depravity, he was portrayed in the 1993 film *Schindler's List*.

Temporary Traffic Control
Wearing a uniform outfitted with the high-visibility traffic control sleeves, a Polish policeman raises his arms as if in surrender as a German soldier snaps his photo while civilians watch from the cobblestoned street's pavement. After Poland's occupation, its pre-war civilian police were mobilised as Blue Police (*Granatowa policja*) and were charged with dealing with regular criminal control as well as smuggling. However, they did not support or take part in the murder of Polish Jews and often served the anti-German resistance at their own peril.

Transition of Traffic Control Power
Directing traffic in Warsaw, a member of the German *polizei* has taken control of the streets.

On Foot Patrol in Poland
As a soldier out of frame to their right gives the Hitler salute, a troop of *Schutzpolizei* march out from their barracks in occupied Poland. Some police elements took part in the Third Reich's wholesale murder of some 2.5 million Catholic Poles, focusing on the intelligentsia, clergy and military officers, as well as helping to orchestrate the death of another 3 million of the country's Jewish population, with men, women and children being sent to the death camps set up in Poland, including Auschwitz.

Above left: **Mounted Policeman**
Wearing two-toned riding breeches, early 'crushed' service cap and spur-equipped boots of the horse-mounted police, an officer seems unflappable even as the wind disturbs the tunic that displays a sports badge and a War Merit Cross award ribbon.

Above right: **Police Horse, Jasło, Poland**
A member of the German police, perhaps the 5th Police Calvary Battalion, poses with his riding mount. Notations on the reverse of the photograph indicate it was taken in the rural city of Jasło, located in south-eastern Poland. Nearby was the Szebnie concentration camp, where many of Jasło's Jews died, though the majority were sent to the Bełżec death camp. The town was completely destroyed when German forces fled the Red Army's advance.

House Search, Poland, 1939
The notation on this commercially printed German postcard describes horse-mounted SS police as investigating 'a murder by fire' that occurred at a Polish farmstead. One SS-*Polizei* brandishes a Luger pistol. The photo postcard was issued during the War Winter Relief drive of 1939/40 as one of a series chronicling the 'Actions of our Police in the East'.

Round-up of Jews, Poland, September 1939
A series of 'snapshots' taken by a German mounted policeman document the attack upon a Jewish village, its 'evacuation' of men, women and children, and their final destination. Notations on the back of the photographs date them as having been taken 2–3 September 1941, the *aktion* launched immediately after the first day of the attack on Poland on 1 September. The soldiers can be seen resting on the right after having set the wooden homes ablaze.

'Evacuation', September 1939
The villagers are marched away as German troops on foot, horseback and bicycles move further into Polish territory. The executions teams moved methodically among the hundreds of small villages (*shtetls*) and the scope of the murders could range from two or three victims to hundreds. No killing action was seen as too small or too larger as total annihilation was the directive.

The Final Destination, September 1939
The prisoners have been brought to a forest-lined field and forced to lie in the sun without food or water, a common practice to 'condition' prisoners to prevent any resistance and make the victims more compliant during the execution process. This was the last of the group of photos taken by the soldier. Official regulations prohibited photos of executions; however, German soldiers, often carrying their own cameras, frequently recorded the scenes, sharing them with friends and family.

Refugees
Caught in the advance of the German
invasion, a Polish Jewish family has been
stopped for a photo, if not more.

**Sunday Edition of the *Illustrierte
Beobachter* Newspaper,
9 November 1939**
Published in Munich, this special edition of
the official Nazi newspaper, the *Illustrated
Observer*, spotlights a photo feature titled
'German Police Bring Order to Poland'.
The scene is the Jewish ghetto established
in Lublin, one of the centres for collecting
Jews prior to the Final Solution. The
photos were recorded by *Kriegsberichters*
(war correspondents) Von Fritz Boegner
and Friedrich Franz Bauer, while the text
was credited to a Kurt von Krazlein.

Against the Wall in the Lublin Ghetto

SS/SD Police at Work
A young polish civilian is searched by an SS/SD *Gefreiter* (corporal) for whatever may incriminate him of any of the various 'crimes' that can validate his imprisonment or worse.

Provocative Photo
Perhaps deliberately chosen for its lurid tone, the photograph appeared with the caption: 'One came upon hundreds of thousands of adolescent boys, made work-shy by years of unemployment and working more and more on criminal activities. Under his clothes are harboured blood-sucking vermin that require an examination by a chemist.' The term 'work-shy' was a catch-all phrase employed by Nazi propagandists to characterise those who did not meet their criteria as productive members of Third Reich society, with them being used as slave labour or else eradicated.

Bringing Order
The newspaper photo caption reads: 'A commando of the Security Police (*Sicherheitspolizei*) has set out to investigate suspicious abandoned houses for lingering pests.' The term 'pest' refers to Jews. The Nazi reference to Jews as vermin was meant to label them a form of disease, justifying their eradication.

Above left: **Racial Profiling**
The photo caption, again espousing Nazi anti-Semitic propaganda's effort to dehumanise and demonise Jews, reads: 'From such Jewish rabble, the hidden and devious killers are recruited.' The photo refers to a reference in the article to the shooting of a Nazi official while riding in his automobile, perhaps the action of Polish resistance fighters. However, the Jews made a more convenient scapegoat as they were more readily available and unarmed. The motivation for the round-up also included the pre-emptive neutralising of any young men fit enough to pose resistance to German occupation.

Above right: **Singled Out**
The photo caption reads: 'Polish Jews, their guilty conscience written on their faces.'

Put to Work
Two German soldiers order an orthodox Polish Jew to fill a pothole. The captions read: (top) 'They are used to woman's work and have not yet learned real work. The ghetto spits them out, the plague of Poland'; and (bottom) 'They don't know physical labour, not even how to handle a shovel.' Later untold thousands would dig their own graves with German shovels as the police death squads swept through Poland, Eastern Europe and Russia.

Arbeit Macht Frei
A work detail is led through a rubble-strewn street, the men's clothing bearing the mandatory yellow Star of David. Caught without them meant execution. If anyone managed to escape from a labour camp, when captured they were forced to work to pay for the bullets used to kill them.

***Above left*: Non-Innocent Bystanders**
German soldiers enjoy mocking a Polish Jew pressed into forced labour. The complicity of the regular army in the Holocaust was denied for decades, with the blame laid at the feet of the SS until more recent research and public exhibitions in Germany established the army's widespread cooperation and facilitation of atrocities.

***Above right*: Souvenir Photo**
Invoking the Nazi racist mindset relating to the 'subhuman' status of Poles in general and Jews in particular, German soldiers often took such photos to send home, 'authenticating' the validity of their 'cleansing' operations in Eastern Europe.

Above left: **Mandatory Armbands**
In a soldier's album, a photo is neatly captioned 'Polish Jews.' The opened windows seem to indicate the warmth of summer. While the older man looks away from the German's camera, the young boy can't resist smiling, while a young girl with a ribbon in her hair looks on. Next to the boy a German communication (*Nachtrichten*) vehicle can be glimpsed. In fact, the photo was dated in the summer of 1941 by a member of a Wehrmacht communications group that was on its way through Eastern Europe to join in the invasion of the Soviet Union.

Above right: **Caught on the Road to 'Resettlement'**
A German camera focuses on a Polish Jewish family, each carrying the maximum allowance of personal belongings permitted during their deportations, unaware that at their ultimate destination their luggage will be confiscated, along with their lives. Jews as a source of revenue was a major component in the Nazi plan to exterminate them while appropriating their property and valuables.

Curiosity
A German corporal grins for the camera as he stands next to his prisoner, the Jewish boy perhaps selected to pose for the camera because of his height.

Polish Volunteers
Wearing armbands identifying them as security adjuncts of the Wehrmacht, a group of smiling Polish policemen pose for a German camera. After Polish policemen were forcibly recruited into German-controlled *Polnisches Schutzmannschaftsbataillon* 202, some 360 men were sent to the east. However, most deserted to join the Polish 27th Home Army Infantry Division, fighting the German-sponsored Ukrainian Insurgent Army (UPA) – the latter intent on purging all non-Ukrainians from areas of Poland they considered Ukrainian territory. The nationalist forces, with the aid of local Ukrainian peasants, murdered as many as 100,000 Poles – mostly women and children, often by torture – in an act of non-German genocidal ethnic cleansing. The attacks against Poles continued even into the last weeks of the war. However, if any Ukrainian policeman in service to the Germans deserted, German retaliation included the murder of the individual's family and destruction of his village. These actions were carried out by Polish policemen. In the exchange of violence on both sides, subsequent death tolls for Ukrainians as the result of Polish revenge are estimated at 10 to 20,000, the killings occurring both during the war and post-war.

Poland: 'Partisans' Captured
With one policeman leading in front and a second joined by a non-German auxiliary, the four prisoners, a woman and three men, are led through the snow to an unknown destination. Notations on the reverse identify the civilians as 'partisans' – a catch-all term meaning that any such listed could be subject to execution. While being the location chosen by Germans to establish their extermination camps, Poland was the only occupied or Axis country not to take an organised part in the Holocaust. Many Poles hid Jews and lost their lives as a result. However, anti-Semitism was endemic in Poland and many individuals betrayed Jews for rewards. Moreover, many enthusiastically took part in taking over or looting their homes and businesses, then refused to return them at war's end. In several instances Polish civilians attacked and killed former Jewish concentration camp prisoners trying to return home.

Above left: Captured for the Camera
Polish auxiliaries have joined in the German round-ups of Jews, in this case city dwellers. The 'souvenir' photo taken in Poland bears a single handwritten notation on the reverse in German – *Juden*. The prisoners' fate is almost certain. Execution squads had begun shooting Jewish civilians in the very first week of the Polish invasion.

Above right: Permanently Barred Doors
Four soldiers posed by the decorated doors of an orthodox Jewish house of worship. It is unlikely they can translate the Hebrew that indicates the entrance is reserved for the entry of female worshippers. The photo is dated 20 February 1940, some six months after the invasion of Poland.

Racial Cleansing
A German soldier has chosen to record the destruction of a Jewish synagogue. When conducting a 'cleansing' action in a small town or village, the victims were often packed into barns, synagogues or other available buildings and burned to death, a common modus operandi with a practical consideration; namely, to conserve ammunition as well as to inflict the maximum amount of pain on the victims. Occasionally synagogues were also converted into horse stables or brothels.

***Above left*: 'Polnische Juden'**
Polish Jews are gathered together under the casual control of three unarmed German soldiers. One woman glares steadfastly into the camera, her ultimate fate unknown.

***Above right*: Lifecycle and the First to Die**
Police units helped transport Jews into the various ghettos established across Europe, the carefully orchestrated step prior to conveyance to the death camps in Poland. A vast network of railway lines were developed to feed the extermination centres, their cargo often superseding priority over regular German troop transports. Once the trains arrived, the first to be gassed were the very old and the very young; thus, post-war photos of piles of corpses show only young adults, who had been kept for a period as slave labour. Cold statistics estimate over 1.5 million children were killed.

Kielce, Poland: *Judisches Wohnviertel* – Echo of Crimes
A barbed wired-encrusted sign posted in German, Polish and Hebrew translates euphemistically to 'Jewish Residential Area'. The pre-war Jewish population of Kielce numbered some 22,000, swollen by an additional 6,000 Jews who fled to the city as the German threat grew, with 28,000 eventually being trapped there after the town's occupation on 4 September 1939. The final liquidation of the ghetto was carried out during 20–24 August 1942 by the Germans with the aid of Ukrainian, Lithuanian and Polish volunteers. The elderly, invalids and the ill were shot on the spot. The remaining 19,000 Kielce Ghetto Jews were sent by train to Treblinka for immediate extermination.

Above left: **Death Train**
Jewish civilians, including children, peer out from a German transport train in Poland. Given no food or water, with no sanitation and drained by summer heat reaching over 100° F or frozen by winter temperatures falling to -20° F, many were killed on the way to the concentration camps. Often with more than 100 people packed like sardines into each car, when the doors were opened they were often filled with corpses. People were so tightly packed that there was often no room even for the dead to fall to the floor, with the corpses remaining standing with the living.

Above right: **Unscheduled Deaths in Poland**
Corpses of men and women litter a railroad track, the debris scattered around their bodies indicating they have been searched for valuables. In post-war Poland, those who rescued Jews kept it a secret in fear of reprisal from their neighbours as a result of the intense level of residual anti-Semitism, but also prompted by the belief that anyone who hid Jews had accrued money and valuable items in exchange, and thereby now became a prime target for robbery. Shortly after the death camps in Poland were liberated, local civilians turned the areas into moonscapes by frenzied digging in the soil looking for 'Jewish plunder'. To aid their search away from the prying eyes of competitors, the scavengers often took home entire skulls in order to check for gold teeth.

Kalisz, Poland: Execution of a Priest, November 1939
This series of photos was printed on a post-war commercial Polish postcard, one of several that graphically chronicled the German occupation. Note the large audience of German soldiers watching from grandstands as police lead the blindfolded clergyman to his death. Located in central Poland, Kalisz is considered the country's oldest city. Located on the Polish–German border, it was quickly captured at the outset of the war with little fighting. Along with some 30,000 of the area's Jews, 20,000 local Catholics were either murdered or expelled as slave workers as part of the Nazi plan to obliterate Polish national identity and culture.

Kraków, Poland: Comradeship, 1941
Enjoying beer and a songfest, several dozen policemen, including one visibly wearing SS runes on his uniform, relax while on assignment in Kraków, Poland.

On 6 June 1942, German police and SS troops liquidated the Krakow Ghetto. Sweeping through its streets, they killed 600 bedridden and disabled people, as well as anyone attempting to flee. The survivors were deported via railway cars, with some 6,000 Jews being sent to the Belzec extermination camp. It was in Kraków that Sudeten German, successful businessman and Nazi party member Oscar Schindler of *Schindler's List* fame, operated the enamelware factory that became a refuge for Jews, with Schindler saving many hundreds from death. On 11 August 1945, three months after the war had ended, anti-Jewish riots erupted in Kraków. Jews were also attacked and killed in other Polish towns and cities – a matter of historical record that modern Poland still deals with.

Liquidation of the 'Asocials and Undersirables'

Victims of *Porraimos*
A German soldier's camera captures the images of three *Zigeuner,* or gypsy children. Nazi racial policies condemned the Roma, Sinti and Lalleri peoples to the fate suffered by its Jewish victims – persecution, arbitrary internment, forced labour and mass murder. The SS and police took part in the rounding up of gypsies, deporting them to labour and death camps, as well as carrying out mass executions on the spot. While there were some exceptions afforded to the gypsies, for example distinguished First World War military service, even those currently in the German Wehrmacht were often seized while on leave. The word *Porraimos* ('The Devouring') is used to describe the gypsy holocaust, also known as 'The Great Sadness'.

Family Group
Some 23,000 Roma, Sinti and Lalleri
were sent to Auschwitz, where Mengele
was fond of using them for his medical
experiments. While the German guards
found the gypsies entertaining and treated
them less harshly than other prisoners, in
May 1944 word reached them that the
entire so-called 'Gypsy Family' compound
was to be exterminated. There was
resistance, but it was futile. In the end at
least 19,000 of the 23,000 Roma sent to
Auschwitz died there, with mothers, fathers
and children often being gassed together.

His Fortune Told, Hers Foretold
With cattle cars to the death camps
visible in the background, German
soldiers appear to have their palms read
by a Roma woman, perhaps hoping to
postpone her own fate. For decades the
post-war West German government
refused to acknowledge the mass murder
of the gypsies as a racially motivated war
crime, preferring to describe their fate as
that suffered by common criminals. Not
until 1979 did the West German Federal
Parliament create eligibility for Roma to
apply for compensation. However, most of
the eligible had already died.

The Balkans: Sinti Sister and Brother
German military and SS police units shot an estimated
30,000 Roma in the Baltic States (Estonia, Latvia,
Lithuania) and elsewhere in the occupied Soviet Union.
The deportations and killings extended throughout
Europe, often with the aid of local collaborators. In
total, estimates of the number murdered range to 25
per cent of all European Roma – some 220,000. Other
estimates range much higher, with as many as 750,000
estimated as having been murdered, since records were
less well kept or recovered.

The Balkans Besieged

Greek Graveyard – Compressed Death
A policeman inspects boxes containing the remains of the deceased. A skull is visible in one open container and has attracted his attention. Because of limited burial space, it was a common practice to place the deceased's bones into the smallest possible container. Each year the deteriorating remains were disinterred and then compressed into a smaller box in order to make more room. If no relative appeared to re-box the remains, the bones were destroyed. The Greek Orthodox Church considered cremation illegal and a bar to the afterlife. During the German occupation, Greek graveyards experienced an even greater overflow. Two of the boxes are inscribed with the dates of 1937 and 1939, prior to the German occupation.

Goebbels and Speer Visit Athens, 1939
An official German press photo dated 1 April 1939 shows Hitler's architect, Albert Speer, apparently pointing out the historical sights of the Greek capital to the Reich Minister of Propaganda several months before the September invasion of Poland. In 1941 German forces invaded Greece after their Italian allies failed in their efforts to occupy Balkan territory, including Yugoslavia and Greece. Hitler had tried to restrain Mussolini from such actions, but il Duce eventually launched the assault, seeking to realise his dream of a new Roman Empire. The Italians met stiff Greek resistance and suffered heavy losses. Coming to Mussolini's aid and thus critically delaying his plans to attack the USSR, German forces struck in early April 1941 and by the end of May had occupied Greece.

Athens: Tourists at the Acropolis, 1942
Standing at the pillars of the Parthenon, German *Gebirgsjäger* (elite mountain troops) take in a lecture by an officer, presumably concerning Greek history. An estimated 300,000 Greek civilians would later die from mass starvation. During the 1941–45 occupation, 460 Greek villages were destroyed and approximately 60,000 men, women and children were killed. In addition, some 65,000 of Greece's 75,000 Jews were killed in Auschwitz. None of the murderers in Greece was ever tried by a German court. Post-war efforts to compensate the Greek villagers were challenged by the German government in 2008, followed in 2012 when the International Court of Justice dismissed the judgment against Germany.

Willing Hands – Eastern Accomplices

Slovenia: Comrade in Training
A rather causal-looking German *polizei* greets a foreign volunteer SS policeman, possibly a Slovenian, who seems to have snapped to attention. The Germans found sufficient numbers of 'volunteers' in occupied territories eager to take part in the systematic murder of their Jewish countrymen.

Slovakian Police Units March in Review for their German Overseers
It appears that one of the volunteers has donned a German helmet while his comrades wear the standard Slovak military issue helmet. One is giving the Hitler salute. In the background, a German officer can be seen watching the proceedings, while in the foreground a briefcase indicates the placement of the cameraman. Among the German forces invading Slovakia were the 4th SS Police Regiment. Having initially performed security duties in occupied France and later composed of both Germans and indigenous volunteers, after being transferred in part to Poland they engaged in anti-partisan actions.

In March 1939, Czechoslovakia as a country was dissolved, the region of Slovakia declaring itself a 'republic' and joining Nazi Germany as an ally on both the battlefield and in the war against the Jews. As a result, some 75,000 Slovakian Jews were rounded up for 'special handling'. The Germans also required the Slovak puppet regime to 'reimburse' the Nazi state 500 Reichsmarks for every Jew sent for 'retraining and accommodation' – another euphemism for murder. German police units and local collaborators took part in wholesale massacres, including the complete destruction of ninety-three Slovakian villages.

Lithuanian Police
Handwritten notations in Lithuanian on the reverse identify the two policemen as the brothers Gintalai. Shoulder strap emblems indicate the 7th Battalion, which was formed in Kaunas after the German occupation.

The notorious 12th Lithuanian Police Auxiliary Battalion was formed in Kaunas in 1941 entirely of volunteers. Later dispatched under German control to Belarus on 5 October 1941, the unit targeted local resistance and partisan groups. The mass murder of Jews was first tested in this area of Byelorussia. The unit's operations centred on the city of Minsk and its surrounding districts, with massacres of civilians being conducted in Slutsk, Smilovichi, Borisov, Rudensk, Koidanov and many other small villages. Its toll included at least 42,000 victims – Jews, partisans, and alleged Communist Party members. As a result of the German occupation, 95 per cent of Lithuanian Jews, some 140,000 in all, were killed, at least half by their own countrymen.

1930s Lithuanian Soldier
The southernmost of the three Baltic States, Lithuania suffered both
under Soviet rule and Nazi occupation. Tracing its history back to
1253 and a long subjugation by Russia, it declared its independence
in 1918. However, in 1940 it was reoccupied by the Soviet troops,
before they were then replaced by German occupiers. In response
to the often brutal and murderous communist oppression, the
Lithuanians embraced the Germans as liberators. While its Jewish
citizens had historically supported independence and fought for their
country against Russian attacks, in the late 1930s laws protecting
their rights were withdrawn. Lithuanian nationalist and anti-Semitic
groups targeted them, further inflamed by Nazi rhetoric. With the
fleeing of Soviet troops as German forces took control, the Jews
were set upon often with a level of barbaric brutality that stunned
even the Germans.

**Latvian Army Soldiers,
Summer 1941**
During the June 1941 invasion
of the USSR, the German forces
were greeted by Latvians as
liberators from Stalinist tyranny.

**German Police
Battalion in Latvia**
The original designation numbers
allocated to police battalions
assigned to Latvia were 16–30,
but this later increased. Reserve
Police Battalion 33 ('Ostland')
conducted actions in Latvia
from August to October 1941.
It would then be sent to Poland,
where the members of its 1st
Company shot 23,000 Jewish
residents of the town of Rowne,
before moving into the Ukraine,
where it murdered many
more thousands.

On the Road outside Riga

Bodies of civilians litter a forested Latvian roadside. A well-dressed man has been shot at close range in the head, his belongings piled on his chest.

Upon invading the Baltic countries in June 1941 on their way into the Soviet Union, the Germans quickly overran Latvia, soon concentrating Latvian Jews in the capital city of Riga. During 7–9 December 1941 (while Pearl Harbor was attacked by the Japanese), the initial rampage against Riga's Jews was initiated by Latvian civilians, who brutally murdered several thousand before the SS police forces of *Einsatzgruppen* A were able to transport by bus some 27,000 men, women and children to the nearby Rumbula Forest, where they were systematically shot with the aid of Latvian volunteers. As a prelude to the mass execution, the SS entered the Riga Ghetto hospital and threw some thirty Jewish babies from the upper windows to their death as their mothers watched.

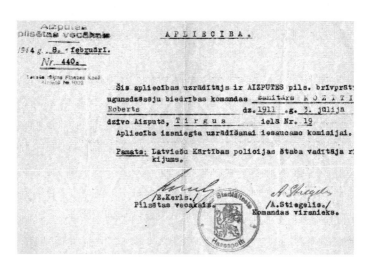

Application for Membership in Latvian SS, 1944

A thirty-three-year-old Latvian named Roberts Rozitis has applied as a medic in the *Lettische SS-Freiwilligen Legion*, the form having been filled out in Riga on 4 February 1944. This date coincides with the expansion of the Latvian formations in January 1944. They eventually faced Soviet forces in the last battles of the war.

On 23 January 1943, Hitler had ordered SS leader Heinrich Himmler to form a Voluntary Latvian SS Legion. When this February application was signed, the Germans still occupied Latvia but were fighting to halt the Soviet advance. In March, the second Latvian SS Legion (19th Division) was formed, which then joined with the former unit to face Soviet forces on 16 March in the battle of the Velikaya River, which later became memorialised as the Legion's Memorial Day in post-war Latvian celebrations. Russian forces re-entered the country in July 1944 and by 13 October 1944 occupied Riga. While some 150,000 Latvians had previously been evacuated to German-controlled territory, another 14,000 Latvian POWs were deported to Siberia. During the see-sawing occupations by the Soviets, the Germans and then the Soviets again, some 300,000 Latvians died. Post-war, some 120,000 Latvians chose to remain in the west.

Cuffs – Latvian Police
With backing from their Nazi allies, the collaborationist organisation Thunder Cross (*Perkonkrusts*) was formed by Latvian fascist Viktor Arajs. As Latvians began serving in the *Ordnungspolizei* and Waffen-SS. Within six months those German-led murder units, including the notorious 21st Latvian Police Division, had killed 90 per cent of Latvia's Jews – some 95,000 men, women and children.

Ukrainian Civilians Transform into German Volunteers
Apparently their blue eyes and blond hair affect an Aryan appearance that aided in their selection by their German masters. While some 4.5 million Ukrainians fought in the Red Army against the German invaders, and with a quarter million joining the partisans, many also chose to don the German uniform and join the Nazis in the hopes of freeing their homeland from the yoke of Stalinist tyranny. Some also shared a racist, often bloodthirsty attitude toward their own Jewish population. Others simply sought financial reward, extra food and alcohol.

Schutzmannschaft – German-Supervised Auxiliary Police

As the Nazi viewed the Slavs as disposable subhumans and treated them as such, the Ukrainians soon took up arms against their occupiers. While many Ukrainians eventually joined anti-Nazi partisan groups, some remained loyal to the Nazi and anti-Soviet cause, some actively and enthusiastically serving in the killing squads hunting down and killing Jews. Many also served as concentration and death camp personnel. For example, approximately thirty-five to forty German SS and police staffed Treblinka, with another ninety to 120 Ukrainians serving as guards. During July 1942 to August 1943 an estimated 900,000 Jewish men, women and children were fed into the death camp's gas and flame.

German *Ordnungspolizei* Pose with Ukrainian 'Protection Forces' in Zarig near Kiev, 1 December 1942 (Signage in Ukrainian and German)

By the end of 1942 there were some 70,000 police stations in the Ukraine. Seen here is a German *Hauptwachtmeister* (sergeant major), identified as Volkman, meeting with the commander of the post, an officer identified as Grosch. Standing nearby in their black uniforms are two members of the Ukrainian collaborationist auxiliary police (*Schutzmannshaft*), the organisation established by Himmler with a ratio of one German to ten local police. In addition to separately formed all-German SS police battalions, some 200 units of 500 volunteers each formed the auxiliary *Schutzmannschaft* Police Battalions, operating within the Ukraine, Belorussia, Latvia, Estonia and Lithuania. Both organisations were directly responsible for anti-partisan warfare but also conducted the mass execution of Jewish civilians whenever and wherever directed. Many years later, after the fall of the Soviet Union, various Eastern European countries began 'rehabilitating' Nazi era collaborationist mass murderers as national heroes under the guise of their 'anti-communist' war records, including notorious mass killer Petro Volnovsky, recently hailed in modern Ukraine.

Above left: **Bulgarian Machine Gun Team**
Joining the Axis alliance in March 1941 after German pressure, the Kingdom of Bulgaria, although a home for Jews for some 2,000 years, enacted anti-Jewish measures. In late 1943 the first deportations of non-Bulgarian Jews found in Bulgarian territories began. The German request for payment to cover their costs of the deportation was granted, including fees for the 3,545 adults and 592 children sent to the Treblinka death camp. Another 11,600 followed, all of whom perished. With the aid of Bulgarian military police, German soldiers also engaged in the random killings of Jewish civilians. However, due to protests from Bulgarian politicians, clergy and civilians, and the efforts of King Boris, the country's indigenous Jews, some 48,000, were not given over to the Germans. This was a rare instance where a country stood in unity against the Nazis to save its fellow Jewish citizens, if not its non-citizens – the subject still a matter of controversy.

Above right: **Romanian Traditions**
In traditional dress, civilians greet German troops arriving in their country. When the German police mobile killing units set out to perform their operations, they found the Romanians had already murdered most of their fellow Jewish countrymen, including 150,000 by the Romanian Fourth Army. Additionally adherents of the anti-Jewish right-wing *Esalon Operativ*, during government-initiated 'ethnic cleansing and purification actions' they attacked any and all Jews they could find, often using knives and crowbars. Even the Germans complained about their methods and the tendency to leave the corpses unburied.

Romania: Mass Murder in Odessa
With the largest Jewish population of any Soviet city, Odessa was a prime target. Using a delayed time bombing by the Soviet secret police, the Germans blamed the local Jewish population. 5,000 Jews and communists were immediately hung from lamp posts and telephone poles across the city, shortly followed by 19,000 Jews being shot and doused with petrol, then burned.

By February 1942 Romania was declared *Judenrein*, 'cleansed of Jews'. In total, Romanian soldiers with the aid of German mobile teams took part in the killing of as many as 380,000 men, women and children. In addition, over 25,000 Romanian Sinti and Romani peoples perished during Romania's collaboration with Germany.

An official 2004 Romanian government report concluded: 'Of all the allies of Nazi Germany, Romania bears responsibility for the deaths of more Jews than any country other than Germany itself. The murders committed in Iasi, Odessa, Bogdanovka, Domanovka, and Peciora, for example, were among the most hideous murders committed against Jews anywhere during the Holocaust.'

Hungary: Last Great Gasp of Mass Murder, 1944

Wearing this distinctive 'rooster feathers' headgear, a Hungarian *Gendarmerie* (*Csendőrség*) poses with his German troops. Hungary was a somewhat reluctant ally of Nazi Germany and was particularly resistant in turning over its Jews to the SS. After German forces took over control of the country, they directed Adolf Eichmann to orchestrate the deportation by rail of 438,000 Hungarian Jews. Their destination was Auschwitz, where upon arrival 90 per cent were immediately 'reduced to smoke and dust'. The mission of mass death was accomplished from 19 March 1944 to 6 June 1944, less than three months, with the trains arriving non-stop and the gas chambers working overtime.

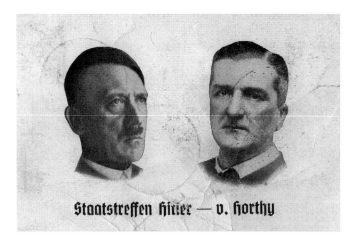

Staatstreffen hitler — v. horthy

German Commercial Postcard Celebrates Meeting between Hitler and Vice-Admiral Horthy, August 1938

While Hungarian gendarmes rounded up Jews in rural areas for collection into ghettos, they often ransacked their homes, even torturing Jews for any valuables. As a result the complicity of the royal Hungarian government is still a controversial subject. Hungary's regent Horthy was seen as opposing Eichmann's murderous plans, although during his 1961 trial testimony Eichmann gave full credit to Hungarian political and police authorities for carrying out the last great mass murder operation of the war. Post-war, the German ambassador to Hungary, Edmund Veesenmeyer, also testified that the deportations would have been impossible without 'the enthusiastic participation of the entire Hungarian police apparatus'.

The Beginning of the End

Above left: **A Policeman's Grim Christmas, 1942**
Standing alongside a vintage cannon, a gaunt policeman faces the camera. At this point the battle at Stalingrad is heading for disaster, the German 6th Army having been encircled by Soviet troops, leading to a major turning point in the war.

Above right: **Elder Policeman – The Tide of War Turning Against Germany, July 1943**
During this month Germany sustained major losses, including the failed assault on Kursk that saw the greatest tank battle of any war. Compounding the German losses, the Allies landed on Sicily and Mussolini is deposed by his own people while an Allied '1,000-plane raid' rained devastation on Hamburg.

Three Veterans, July 1944
All three wear ribbons indicating their participation in campaigns outside the borders of Germany. The man on right wears a Wound Badge in black, indicating one wound. The handwritten notation on the reverse states that the photograph was taken on 2 July 1944 and gives the names of policemen as (left to right) Franz Frister, Willi Koch and Brenken. On this date, Germany is spiralling to defeat on all fronts: in the west the Allies have landed in Normandy, and in the east the Red Army are on the verge of destroying Army Group Centre.

Total War Arrives in Russia

Second Wave, June 1941
Police units following closely behind combat troops enter a Russian town. The German High Command named the invasion of the Soviet Union as Operation Barbarossa after Emperor Frederick Barbarossa of the Holy Roman Empire, a leader of the twelfth-century Third Crusade. On 22 June 1941, German forces attacked with some 3 million soldiers, including Hungarian and Romanian allies, fielding an armada of 3,580 tanks, 7,184 artillery guns, 1,830 planes and 750,000 horses. The storm of fire and steel launched on both land and from the air struck eastward, intent on destroying Stalinist Russia.

Lenin as Gallows
A Russian woman has
been strung up from the
outstretched arm of the
communist founder. A cloth
covers her face and a placard
pinned to her describes her
'crimes'.

As Western Europe's 'cultural
warriors', German soldiers
brought both orchestras
and poison gas. Seeing
themselves as the defenders
of Western civilization
and as crusaders against
the Asiatic hordes of the
Bolshevik-Jewish world threat,
they viewed their victims as
Slavic *untermenschen*, or
subhumans – or as Göring
described them, 'useless eaters'.
Thus once the war had been
won, the Nazi leadership,
in addition to targeting all
communist functionaries
and Jews, scheduled 30
million Russians for mass
extinction via starvation
to make room for German
colonists. The extermination
of the Russian Jewish
population would also open
up room to deposit the mass of
European Jews scheduled for
'special handling.'

'With Hans in Shitomir'
Two bicycle troopers repair a tire in
the summer heat of the Ukraine near a
town called Zhytomyr (spelled Shitomir
in German). Located west of Kiev, the
strategic town was occupied by German
forces in mid-July 1941. Also during this
month, Göring ordered SS leader Heydrich
to send in the *Einsatzgruppen* to implement
the extermination of the Jewish population
in the Ukraine. During the following
September the city, a major centre of Jewish
culture, was accused of aiding partisans,
and was thus visited by the *Einsatzgruppe*
C joined by *Sonderkommando* 4a and
Order Police Battalion 303. Together they
shot 18,000 of the town's Jewish residents,
including many children.

**Ukraine: Round-Up of Jews –
Fate Pre-Determined, 1941**
A German soldier, his shadow
visible to the left, photographs
a closely packed group of boys
and men standing in the center
of what what appears to be a
fenced-in garden. In the left
background a white-coated
Ukrainian volunteer deals with
a smaller group of prisoners.
Others can be glimpsed in the
background, their heads and
caps just visible as they lay on
the ground or huddle in small
groups, waiting their turn for the
next 'selection'.

No Escape
Further magnification reveals
the spectrum of emotions
evident on the prisoners' faces.
The younger men may or may
not be set aside for slave labor,
depending on the executioners'
plan of action.

Luger at the Ready
Standing by a Birch tree in a
Russian forest, a 'partisan' is
photographed. His captor's
pistol and rifles stand ready.

Execution of Duties
Placards attached to the two men claim they are partisans, with the punishment awaiting any others written in both German and Russian. The SS, police and SD often served as hangmen, as did regular army personnel. By 1945 the execution squads had killed some 3 million civilians, including some 1.5 million Jews.

Mass Murder in Eastern Europe and Russia

Smiling Policemen with Guns
When killing actions were in their infancy, and before more effective paradigms were developed, one policeman would take in hand one victim and walk with him or her off into the forest, to a quiet place, isolated from view, and then shoot them with his rifle or pistol, firing to the base of the skull. There was even a term for such a method of execution: *Genickschuss*, or neck shot. Those particularly skilled with the technique were referred to as *Genickschuß- Spezialisten* – 'Neck Shot Specialists'.

'Neck Shot' – Commemorative Plaque at Dachau Concentration Camp Marks Site in Three Languages.
In court testimony given in 1965, the technique was described in connection with the murder of asylum patients deemed unqualified for the Third Reich concept of Aryan perfection. 'They were shot individually. The police short-barrelled pistol, with a 7.65 mm calibre, was used as the means of execution. The victims received a single shot in the back of the neck. The barrel of the pistol was placed between the two ligaments at the base of the neck, facing upward. The shot was supposed to pass out at the forehead so that the bullet would have travelled through the entire length of the brain. If that succeeded, blood and brains splashed out of the pulsating wound and death occurred instantly.'

Poland: Killers Who Named Themselves? – Harvest Festival, 1943

On the reverse side of this photo of three policemen, one of them has neatly typed: 'Erntedankfest Sept. 43 in Radziecho. Rechts Kamerad Schubert, links Wm. Rheinhardt.' The owner of the photo does not name himself, since the photograph was originally pasted into his personal album.

Erntedankfest translates to Harvest Festival, a traditional festive occasion, but in this case it referred to a special action against the local Jewish population. '*Erntefest*' was the code name for the extermination of the last surviving Jews remaining in the Lublin District of the *Generalgouvernement* (occupied Poland) in the fall of 1943.

```
Erntedankfest
Sept.43 in Radziecho
rechts Kamerad
Schubert,links.
Wm.Reinhardt.
```

Neatly Typed

The Germans claimed *Erntefest* was in response to incidents of Jewish resistance and revolt in various camps and ghettos, including the Warsaw Uprising. *Erntefest* began at dawn on 3 November 1943. The Trawniki and Poniatowa labour camps were surrounded by SS and police units, the Jewish prisoners being shot in nearby pits. At the Majdanek/Lublin camp, 17,000 people were shot. To conceal the sound of gunfire and screams of the dying, the Germans played music through loudspeakers at both Majdanek and Trawniki, with the killing operations being completed on schedule in a single day. Two days were required at Poniatowa. In total, approximately 42,000 Jews were killed during *Erntefest*, which the Germans officially lauded as a major success.

Field Work in the Soviet Union, Summer 1941

A First World War veteran wearing a black Wound Badge stands with his younger counterpart in a Russian field. Once their work was completed in Poland, police units moved further east in the wake of the German invasion of Russia, which brought a host of new victims literally under the gun. The year 1941 would be pivotal, with Nazi Germany's military success being seemingly unstoppable, its forces initially sweeping away Red Army defenders. However, time, distance, growing resistance and weather, along with a fatal arrogance, brought grinding setbacks, including the failure to occupy Moscow. Far greater defeats would follow but not before Nazi bullets, bombs and flame had killed at least 30 million Russians, leaving its mark on Soviet national, military and political thought for decades to come.

'3 *Freischärler im Gefangenschaft*' – Two Partisans in Captivity

Alleged Russian 'partisans' have been roped together and led down a dusty village road to their fate. One appears to be a youth, the other an elderly man. Hidden from view, the legs of a small boy are visible in front of the cyclist.

The catch-all term partisans included suspected partisan helpers, suspicious individuals, looters, spies, gypsies, Mongols, Armenians, Muslims, Red Army Commissars and Soviet officials, as well as provocateurs, stragglers and others considered 'useless eaters'. The edict of the time was that 'all Jews are partisans and all partisans are Jews', whether or not they were found with weapons.

Partisan in Peril

His face wound bandaged, a Russian prisoner pleads his case with his police captors as one somewhat distractedly stands guard nearby. If judged a partisan, his fate is sealed. After the majority of the Eastern European and Ukrainian Jewish population had been killed, police battalions then found themselves engaging in anti-partisan actions and facing regular Red Army troops.

On Duty in Rotterdam, Holland, Christmas 1940

In a rare photo, members of Field Police Battalion 322 pose before their neatly arrayed holiday gifts.

Rotterdam

On 14 May 1940, while surrender negotiations were taking place, flights of German bombers struck Rotterdam, the resulting firestorm killing 800 to 900 civilians, other reports claiming 25,000 dead. Although its forces fought fiercely in its defence, Holland surrendered six days later. The SS and police, efficiently aided by collaborationist Dutch police, carried out deportation actions against the Netherlands' 140,000 Jewish citizens. Many were first sent to the transit camp Westerbork, but eventually more than 100,000 perished in Auschwitz and Sobibor – a death rate of some 75 per cent.

Above left: **Rotterdam**
PB 322 would later be posted to Yugoslavia, Slovenia and Russia, where the unit is recorded as having participated in the mass murder of Jewish civilians

Above right: **Service Book of Police Battalion 322 Member Georg Heinkel**
In his carefully notated handbook, a member of the Police Battalion 322 logged his personal data – including the birth of his children, one near the very end of the war, as well as his inoculations, rankings and his various postings. Formed in April 1941 from the members of training battalion Vienna-Kagran, as of June 1941 PB 322 became part of Police Regiment Centre. After 22 June 1941 and the invasion of the Soviet Union, Police Battalion 322 was assigned 'security duties' in eastern Poland and Byelorussia.

Police Battalion 322 – Documented Killers
Seen here, PB 322 members pose at a natural rock
formation. A few display Infantry Assault Badges,
indicating a three-day-straight engagement in Battle.
Others wear Iron Cross 2nd Class ribbons and Wound
Badges, perhaps earned in their anti-partisan actions.
Many of the men smile for the camera.

**Second Group Photo and
New Faces, March 1943**
In this photograph, the men are
not wearing their standard-issue
uniform belts and several
appear to look away from the
camera. Vents for what may be a
munitions bunker are visible. At
this point they have taken part in
several *aktions* in Russia.

Netherlands: PB 322 – Forming Up, 1943
Preparing to set out from their barracks, members of PB
322 take a moment to relax, their packs, gear and helmets
stacked and ready. The location is the town of Boxmeer,
located in south-eastern Netherlands.

Overcoming Obstacles
PB 322 members scale a relatively low wall in training. They wear their white denim fatigues over their regular uniforms. PB 322 would engage in anti-partisan fighting in the Smolensk area, and later took part in operations in Serbia. At one point the 322 was renamed the 9th Company of the 3rd Order Police Battalion.

PB 322 at Ease in the East
Members of the unit clown about aboard a farmer's wagon. Destruction is visible in the background.

Mail Call in the Ukraine, 1942
PB 322 members gather around for the distribution of letters and packages from home. The state of their uniforms and helmets indicate considerable action in the field. In the right foreground one policeman's cuff title is visible on his left forearm, the script reading 'Deutsche Wehrmacht', as worn by German police personnel operating alongside units of the Germany Army outside the borders of the Third Reich.

PB 322 – Inferno Unleashed in Russia
According to a notation on the reverse of this photograph, the date is March 1942 and the place is identified as Panowo, where a building described as a bunker burns as a PB 322 member advances toward the flames. Panowo was visited by SS and police units in March of 1942 during the second year of the Russian invasion. Then, as German forces were pushed back by Soviet advances, SS, including Latvian units, rejoined the now retreating defence at Panowo on 7 February 1944. During this month, Germany's Army Group North was decimated, with three German divisions being wiped out.

Aftermath of an *Aktion* at Alexandrowka – Photo by Member of PB 322, 1942
The central hearth of a Ukrainian home and its interlocking log construction are revealed after being set to the torch and flamethrower. The village was the home of Mennonites, an Anabaptist sect founded in Switzerland in the sixteenth century. Its main tenets were pacifism and non-violence.

The Keg is Tapped – PB 322, June 1942
To help relieve the stresses of their work, members of the execution units were encouraged to relax post-*aktions* by listening to music, reading poetry, singing, enjoying their beer, and even playing ping-pong, the game being shipped to them in the field. On June 28 the Germans launched 'Case Blue', targeting Stalingrad and the Caucasus oil fields. While the death squads were still busy with their rifles and machine guns, by this date the first reports had reached the Allies of gas being used to kill Jews.

Gemütlichkeit
Time for some sun and beer. PB 322 members drink from a large stein and mess kit, the wall behind them pockmarked with bullet holes. The German word *Gemütlichkeit* conjures up a feeling of warmth, friendliness and good cheer as well as comradeship, social acceptance and peace of mind. Between July 1941 and July 1942, PB 322 shot to death some 36,700 men, women and children in the areas of Baronvichi, Barssuki, Bialovice, Bialystok, Minsk and Mogilev.

PB 322 in their own Graves
The formation suffered casualties during anti-partisan actions as well from accidents and illness. As a master sergeant eyes the camera, another policeman places a wreath on the coffins. The grave marker is a Christian cross rather than the SS rune, indicating the religious affiliation of the policemen and their civilian roots.

Post-Mortem – Death Cards, Justice and Retribution

Feldgendarmerie Officer with Ambulance

Wounded in Action – Police and SS Convalesce at an Infirmary
Extremely disproportionate figures reported by police anti-partisan forces included high body counts of 'the enemy' and very low numbers of weapons confiscated. Police units recorded even lower casualty rates, further indicating the individuals targeted and killed were most likely unarmed civilians.

Above left: SS Policeman, August 1941
During his civilian life back home in the Bavarian village of Haag, Hans Holler had worked as a bricklayer. Serving in a SS-*Schutzpolizei*, the twenty-one-year-old corporal was killed on 21 August 1941 during the early weeks of the German advance into Russia.

Above right: *Feldgendarmerie* Funeral in Progress
Six policemen carry the large cross-decorated wooden coffin of a comrade apparently following a church service. With most of the Jewish population in occupied territories having been dealt with by early 1944, and with the Red Army advancing relentlessly toward Germany, the police units were redirected to serve in concentration and death camps, anti-partisan campaigns or thrust into front line combat, where they along with all German forces suffered growing losses as the war headed toward disaster for the Third Reich.

Death Card for a Secret Policeman, February 1942
Pictured wearing his Hitler Youth Leader uniform in his memorial card, Emil Martin was a member of the *Geheime Feldpolizei* (Secret Military Police or Gestapo of the army). He died on 26 February 1942 in a reserve hospital on the Eastern Front at the age thirty-five after 'contracting a serious illness'. He was then buried in St Wendel, Germany. The funeral was attended by his wife, Frau Josefa Martin, and son, Heinz Jurgen.

Above left: **Russian SS Cemetery, May 1942**
True to SS ideological fanaticism invoking pagan over Judeo-Christian religious traditions, the Birchwood grave posts are shaped as Nordic runic figures: in this case, the image representing life has been inverted to mean death. A member of the SS-*Schutzpolizei Sturm* II of the 2nd Regiment, Sergeant Paul Hauf died at age thirty-four on 2 May 1942 during the second summer Russian offensive.

Above right: **'Pray for me, that I also die for you!', February 1944**
Georg Sandmair, a *Schutzpolizei Oberwachtmeister* (Master Sergeant), was listed as KIA 'in the east' on 23 February 1944 at the age of thirty-five. His awards included the Iron Cross 2nd Class, War Cross and Wound Badge in black. Sandmair was born in Friedberg in the southern part of Germany, near Augsburg and Munich.

As the war grinds into its final year, the Red Army is devastating whole German armies on the Eastern Front and the Allies have landed in Normandy. Total German military losses on the Eastern Front by the end of 1944 surpassed 1 million killed.

Gebets-Andenken an den Krieger – 'Prayer Keepsake of the Warrior Killed by Bandits', 23 November 1944
A precinct master sergeant in the Municipal Police Force and a veteran of the campaigns in Norway, Yugoslavia, Finland and Greece, Rudolf Heigl, according to his death notice, was killed 'in a surprise attack by bandits while on leave'. The term 'bandits' was used by the Germans when referring to members of the resistance or partisans, the criminal connotation providing an excuse for summary execution.

Fate of Two *Polizei*
Somewhere in a Russian snowfield, the bodies of two policemen lay side by side, one clearly having been shot at close range in the head. The positions of their bodies and point-blank face wounds indicate they were executed, the Russians regarding the police members with particular hatred.

Above left: **Exhumation in Sierpów bei Ozorków, Poland**
This very rare group of photographs was part of a German soldier's personal album. It documents the disinterment by members of the police of a grave site in the central Polish village of Sierpów, near Lodz.

The village of Sierpów, located some 4 miles north of Ozorków, was renamed Brunnstadt during the 1943–45 German occupation. A third of its population was Jewish, who were all murdered, and its two historic synagogues were burned by German troops, who forced the local Jews to demolish the remaining walls. Over 5,000 were eventually killed locally or were sent to death camps, including all children below the age of ten.

Above right: **Coffins Uncovered**
What appear to be eleven wooden coffins have been uncovered. German soldiers, Polish labourers and civilians observe the scene. The circumstances of the German deaths are unknown, but likely occurred in the early days of the 1939 invasion of Poland.

Of Interest to a High Command Staff Officer
A German general inspects one of the disinterred corpses. Notations on the photograph indicate the officer is Walter Petzel, who in 1939 was a German Army Corp I Artillery General operating in Poland. Petzel led one of the first battles of the invasion on 1–3 September. Though initially repulsed by Polish forces, on the third day, by using civilians as human shields, the Germans broke through, but both sides suffered heavy casualties. Petzel survived the war, dying in 1965 at age eighty-four in Hameln in Lower Saxony.

Exhumation Complete
As a civilian makes a notation, a German policeman, cigarette in hand, ponders the corpse of one of the disinterred coffins. Its German uniform insignia indicates the individual was a corporal. The standing dark-clothed civilian wears a *Hilfsarbeiter* armband identifying him as a Polish 'volunteer labourer'.

Postscript Policemen
As seen in a British Information Agency press photo, a rifle-toting British soldier walks directly between two German policemen, his body language indicating his attitude towards the individuals, who until perhaps a few days earlier had been enforcers of the Third Reich. They in turn ignore him and focus on the cameraman taking their photo. An American Jeep can be seen in the background. Due to manpower shortages and the need for German-speaking guards, German policemen were frequently enlisted by the Allies to maintain order among their fellow POWs and German civilians.

Back on Duty, 1949
Once again wearing the traditional shako helmet of the civilian German police, two West German officers are seen in a news photo, which was printed with a caption describing the return of horses looted from a farm. According to the news report, about forty Soviet Zone police, armed with carbines, crossed into the British sector of Berlin on 29 April 1949 and looted a farm near the boundary zones. The Russians were said to have taken cattle, pigs, horses, sheep and other livestock from a farm known as 'Carolinenen Hoehe'. The policemen seen in the photograph were sent to guard the farm, from which twelve horses had also broken away. They were later recovered, including the one seen in the photograph.

A Smiling Policeman Only Pretends to be Behind Bars
In a summary hard to comprehend, some 3,000 men killed at least 1 million human beings in approximately two years' time. Of the many thousands of others who took part directly or indirectly in the mass murders, Germans and volunteers alike, only some hundred were brought to trial. Many received much reduced sentences, with the rest escaping justice to live out their lives unhindered.

Suggested Reading
and Select Bibliography

Blood, Philip W., *Hitler's Bandit Hunters: The SS and the Nazi Occupation of Europe* (Dulles, VA: Potomac Books, 2006).

Browning, Christopher R., *Ordinary Men – Reserve Police Battalion 101 and the Final Solution in Poland* (New York, NY: Harper Collins Publishers, 1992).

Burleigh, Michael, *The Third Reich – A New History* (New York: Hill and Wang, 2000).

Dawson, Robert, *The Porraimos: Photos of the Gypsy Holocaust in World War 2* (England: Alfreton, 2013).

Desbois, Father Patrick, *The Holocaust by Bullets* (New York, NY: Palgrave MacMillan, 2008).

Garson, Paul, *Album of the Damned: Snapshots from the Third Reich* (Chicago Academy Publishers, 2008).

Garson, Paul, *New Images of Nazi Germany – A Photographic Collection* (Jefferson, NC and London: McFarland & Co., 2012).

Gilbert, Martin, *The Routledge Atlas of the Holocaust* (3rd edition) (London: 2002).

Goldhagen, Daniel Jonah, *Hitler's Willing Executioners – Ordinary German and the Holocaust* (New York: First Vintage Books, 1997).

Ed: Hamburg Institute for Social Research, *The German Army and Genocide – Crimes Against War Prisoners, Jews, and Other Civilians, 1939–44* (New York, NY: The New Press, 1999).

Hatheway, Jay, *In Perfect Formation, SS Ideology and the SS-Junkerschule-Todz* (Atglen, PA: Schiffer Military History, 1999).

Hillberg, Raul, *Perpetrators, Victims, Bystanders – The Jewish Catastrophe 1933-45* (New York, NY: Harper Collins, 1992).

Johnson, Eric A., and Karl-Heinz Reuband, *What We Knew – Terror, Mass Murder, and Everyday Life in Nazi Germany – An Oral History* (Basic Books, 2005).

Langerbein, Hans, *Hitler's Death Squads: The Logic of Mass Murder* (Texas A&M, 2004).

Lukas, Richard C., *Did the Children Cry: Hitler's War Against Jewish and Polish Children 1939–45* (New York, NY: Hippocrene Books, 1994).

Megargee, Geoffrey P., *War of Annihilation: Combat and Genocide on the Eastern Front, 1941* (New York, NY: Roman & Littlefield, 2007).

Munoz, Antonio J., *Hitler's Green Army: The German Order Police and their European Auxiliaries 1933–45, Western Europe and Scandinavia* (Bayside, NY: Europa Books Inc., 2005).

Munoz, Antonio J., *Hitler's Green Army: The German Order Police and their European Auxiliaries 1933–45, Eastern Europe and the Balkans* (Bayside, NY: Europa Books Inc., 2006).

Munoz, Antonio J., *Generalgouvernement – Internal Security of the Eastern Occupied Polish Territories 1939–45* (Bayside, NY: Europa Books Inc., 2006).

Poliakov, Leon, *Harvest of Hate – The Nazi Program for the Destruction of the Jews of Europe* (New York, NY: Holocaust Library, 1979).

Pontolillo, James, *Murderous Elite – The Waffen-SS and Its Complete Record of War Crimes* (Stockholm: Leander & Ekholm Publishing, 2009).

Puekert, Detllve J. K., *Inside Nazi Germany – Conformity, Opposition, and Racism in Everyday Life* (London and New Haven: Yale University Press, 1987).

Rhodes, Richard, *Masters of Death- The SS-Einsatzgruppen and the Invention of the Holocaust* (New York, NY: Vintage Books, 2003).

Snyder, Louis L., *Encyclopedia of the Third Reich* (UK, Cumberland House: Wordsworth Military Library, 1998).

Speer, Albert, *Inside the Third Reich* (New York, NY: Avon, 1970).

Syndor, Jr. and W. Charles, *Soldiers of Destruction: The SS Death's Head Division 1939–45* (Princeton, NJ: Princeton University Press, 1977).

Weber, Louis, *The Holocaust Chronicle* (Lincolnwood, IL: Publications International, 2001).

Westermann, Edward B., *Hitler's Police Battalions: Enforcing Racial War in the East* (Lawrence, Kansas: University of Kansas Press, 2005).

Williamson, Gordon, *German Army Elite Units 1939–45* (UK, Elms Court: Osprey Publishing, 1999).

Williamson, Gordon, *Germany Security and Police Soldier 1939–45* (UK, Elms Court: Osprey Publishing, 2002).

Williamson, Gordon, *The SS: Hitler's Instrument of Terror* (New York, NY: Barnes & Noble, 2006).

About the Author

Paul Garson is a freelance journalist and photographer based in Los Angeles, California. He has also written *Two-Wheeled Blitzkrieg* and *Warhorses of Germany* for Amberley Publishing and five additional fiction and non-fiction titles for publishers such as Doubleday and Simon & Schuster, as well as more than 2,500 magazine articles for publications including the *Los Angeles Times*.